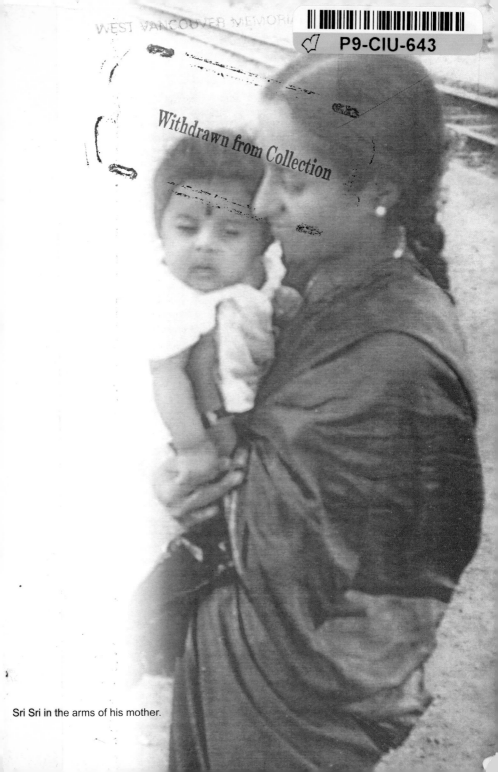

Sri Sri in the arms of his mother.

A young Sri Sri meditating

Sri Sri with Pitaji & Bhanu

Sri Sri with his mother.

Sri Sri with his mother on his right, and sister Bhanu, on his left.

Kids of the Art Excel Dance troupe with Guruji

Thousands greet The Guru of Joy wherever he goes

Sri Sri doing *aarti*: rediscovering the inner meaning of the art of *puja*.

Sri Sri in a moment of celebration.

Sri Sri performing a *puja* in Kolkatta.

Indu Jain, Chairwoman of the *Times of India* group, with Sri Sri

Thousands doing The Mahakriya in Kerala

The ancient and the new come together

Guruji in meditation

THE GURU OF JOY

Sri Sri Ravi Shankar
The Art & of Living

an imprint of
The India Today Group
New Delhi

THE GURU OF JOY

Sri Sri Ravi Shankar
The Art of Living

Sri Sri Ravi Shankar
was born on 13 May, 1956, in a religious family in
Papanasam, Tamil Nadu. At the age of four, he could recite the entire
Bhagavad Gita and by the time he was nine years old, he had mastered the *Rig-Veda*. He
completed his traditional studies, including an advanced degree in modern science, before being
noticed in 1975 by Maharishi Mahesh Yogi, the guru responsible for introducing meditation to
the West. Maharishi took the promising youngster with him to Delhi, Rishikesh, as well as
broad. In 1982, after having decided to strike it on his own, Sri Sri Ravi Shankar went into ten
days of silence. It was during this silence that the *Sudarshan Kriya*, a unique cleansing and
rejuvenating process based on the repetition of different breathing rhythms, was revealed to
him. And so the Art of Living was born. Today the AOL Basic Course, a combination of
pranayama, course points, meditation and group techniques, is taught in
140 countries and Sri Sri Ravi Shankar is a world renowned spiritual master,
as well as a founding member, along with several world leaders, of the
International Association for Human Values (IAHV), a Geneva based organization that
aims to re-awaken human values. He has been a featured speaker at many forums
across the globe including the European Parliament, the
United Nations Millennium Summit and the World Economic Forum
in Davos, Swizerland.

First published in India by
Ashok Chopra
Books Today
The India Today Group
1A, Hamilton House,
Connaught Place,
New Delhi-110 001

© 2002, François Gautier
who asserts the moral right to be
identified as the author of this work.

First published   2002
First reprint   2002
Second reprint   2003
Third reprint   2003

Photographs :   Pramod Pushkarna, Saibal Das,
                 Bhaskar Paul, Soumitra Ghosh,
                 Hemant Chawla, and Rupinder Khullar

Typeset by Nikita Overseas (P) Ltd.
in Calisto MT 12/14 pts

Printed and bound at
Thomson Press, (India) Ltd.

Dedicated to
all Gurus
present, past and future

Acknowledgement

To Rohini Singh,
who added a professional touch to
this book, while retaining its spirit.

Contents

Contents

Foreword

At a time when many people feel that modern knowledge and ancient traditions tend to contradict each other, it is refreshing to come across someone like Sri Sri Ravi Shankar who has been able to reconcile his scientific education with his Vedic training to find a path relevant to contemporary needs. As a result, he has established the *Art of Living Foundation*, whose avowed aim of encouraging people from all backgrounds, religions and cultural traditions to join together in celebration and service is highly admirable. I have had the pleasure of meeting him several times as well as visiting his *ashram*.

Francois Gautier's longstanding personal and professional interest in India has found expression in this book about Sri Sri Ravi Shankar. I am sure readers who are concerned to find ways to re-awaken human values in their own lives today will find much here to inspire them.

— H.H. The Dalai Lama

A BOAT RIDE IN BENARES

*I*T WAS A BEAUTIFUL NOVEMBER NIGHT, COOL WITHOUT being chilly. The two lean oarsmen had paddled us to the middle of the Ganges and then let the boat slowly drift with the current. A light mist made the faraway lights sparkle mysteriously. The pilgrimage town of Kashi was already asleep and except for a few sadhus huddled around a makeshift fire, nobody was in sight on the banks. The silence, broken only by the prow lapping the water, was absolute, pregnant with a presence. At 9.00 p.m., the moon rose on the horizon, gilding the Ganges with a coat of shimmering silver.

Sri Sri Ravi Shankar was sitting at the bow, draped in white robes, an enigmatic smile on his face. Then, one of the devotees quietly started humming a *bhajan*, as ancient as the city of Kashi itself: "*Om namah Shivaya, Om namah*

Shivaya"; and soon all of us joined him softly, so as not to break the magic spell of the silent silver night. After a moment, Sri Sri closed his eyes and seeing him totally absorbed, perhaps in some mystical realm, touched our souls as nothing else could. An atmosphere of stillness and serenity descended on us. In a corner, a girl started shedding quiet tears of ecstasy; an elderly man joined his hands in a silent prayer, a wordless gesture of deeply felt gratitude; everyone shone with intense inner joy, bliss and wonder. As for me, to my surprise, I realized that the characteristic chattering in my mind had quietened; and my soul soared high in the air. Perfectly in the moment, I savoured every bit of it.

Later, as we were driving back to the hotel, and I was holding this precious experience close to my heart, trying not to let it go, I tried to remember when and how it had all started.

CHAPTER ONE

A SCEPTIC'S TRYST WITH SERENITY

Meditation is seeing GOD in yourself
Love is seeing GOD in the person next to you
Knowledge is seeing GOD everywhere.

*O*NE FINE MORNING, AS I WAS SITTING IN THE GARDEN of my home in Auroville (a city based on Sri Aurobindo's vision) having a cup of tea with my wife Namrita, we received an unexpected visit from our friend, Krishnakant, from Paris. This was his first trip to India after almost five years. An ardent devotee of Sri Aurobindo and the Mother, Krishnakant was keen to know all that had happened in the *ashram* and Auroville during his absence. We were discussing Sri Aurobindo's vision of enlightenment and the supramental, when, in the course of our conversation, Krishnakant observed that I seemed to be facing some discomfort as I kept sneezing. Casually, he mentioned, "Why don't you go to the Art of Living Centre in Bangalore and learn some breathing techniques? It might help."

He then gave me the address of the Centre. I reluctantly took it, put it away and then completely forgot about it. I was cynical and sceptical, because I had been living with this condition since I was six years old, when I was hit on my nose by a heavy steel swing in a fair. It had badly damaged the inner bone and impaired my breathing. And subsequent operations had not helped. Yet, a few months later, I actually thought about what Krishnakant had said; I thought I ought to check it out but once again, my logical mind dissuaded me. I was then writing for *Le Figaro*, France's largest circulated newspaper. Often while working on the computer, I had noticed that my breathing was shallow and I knew that it could only have negative consequences for my body in the long run. Finally, I decided to take the plunge and go to Bangalore with Namrita. Perhaps if I do it, I thought, giving the cause added justification, some important shift might take place in my life and it would rekindle in me the intense spiritual aspiration and innocence I had known during my first years in Pondicherry, when the Mother was still there in Her body.

The next day, Namrita joined me on a flight to Bangalore. We took a taxi from the airport to Gyan Mandir, the Art of Living Centre in Bangalore city. In the car, I was lost in my thoughts, lamenting the state of affairs at work. I wondered whether my editor at *Le*

Figaro would accept what I had written. I silently concluded that all this talk about freedom of the press was humbug. Where was the freedom? I was jolted out of my thoughts by a sudden scream from Namrita. A dog had darted across the road bringing our speeding car to a halt. The driver turned back with a smile, as though to reassure us that everything was under control! He then continued driving in a relaxed manner as if nothing had happened. To calm down a visibly shaken Namrita, I joked that these drivers played a dual role. They were not only drivers but sent to remind us to pray. And they certainly did a better job of it than the catholic priests back home in France, I joked.

Observing the driver who still had a smile on his face and was now humming a tune, I wondered how he could be so relaxed in the midst of all this chaos, where no rule or logic works. These illiterate people seem to have more faith than me, I thought. As I was comparing myself with the people around me, the driver again stopped and exchanged a few words in the local language with a passer-by. I thought he was asking for directions. I admired the friendliness between them, the jokes they were obviously enjoying, an easiness I had not experienced before. We rarely saw this in France, I thought. Have we journalists become too serious? No one encourages us to laugh and have fun — there went my mind galloping on its horse again.

The car stopped once more, this time at our destination.

As it happened, there was an Art of Living Basic Course starting and we simply enrolled. As we entered the venue for the course, I glanced at Namrita, who comes from a rather westernised family, and knew that she was not at all interested. Her path was set, as was her mind. She was doing this only because I had persuaded her to. Our instructor, Michael Fischman, an American, started with, "We all want happiness, love and peace. We fail to realize this because we are stressed. The breathing techniques that we learn here will help to release stress." He went on to explain the laws that govern the seven layers of our existence and the four sources of energy.

As the course progressed, it kindled my interest. I turned around and looked again at my wife. Her reluctance seemed to be easing. I heaved a sigh of relief. I observed the others in the group. They all seemed to be absorbed in the logical explanations given by Michael and in getting in touch with the simple truths of their own lives. My rebellious journalistic mind, however, was still analysing and questioning. But Michael was sweet and seldom put me down. I admired his patience to answer all sorts of questions from this heterogeneous group. Perhaps, if I had been him, I thought, I would have lost my temper. I wondered what made him so poised. Even though what he said made sense, I continued to have a dialogue with myself. At the end of the session, as we were walking out of the venue, reflecting on this point, Arvind, one of the participants, candidly commented, "You know, I am an agnostic, but today, something about the teaching — and the man behind the teaching — has touched me deeply. I have decided to proceed with this course, even though I came here against my will, because my wife forced me to." This declaration moved us more than anything else: if an agnostic, a man who said openly that he enjoyed his drink, and who had been a total sceptic as he had confessed to us, could be touched by these simple "basic" techniques, then there must be something more than we thought to the Art of Living. Thus we decided to quell our doubts and also come back the next day.

And so it was that we found ourselves again in Gyan Mandir the next evening, a little more receptive than we had been on the previous day. However, immediately upon starting the session, Michael gently urged Namrita, who was still holding back, "to give her hundred per cent". She got upset and thought, "what does this man know? I have practised many forms of *pranayama* before in Auroville!" As she was fretting and fuming, she suddenly became aware that the pattern of her breath had changed: it had became shorter and more laboured. It then dawned on her that the breath is indeed the connecting link between the mind and emotions: that when one is anxious, under pressure, or stressed, there is a deviation in the natural rhythm of the breath. With this realization something opened up in her and she decided to "give her hundred per cent" to whatever was to come. And then we experienced the *Sudarshan Kriya*. It was so powerful that it literally "blew my mind". For the first time since I could remember, I became quiet and serene. It was like taking a holiday from my chattering mind; an unusually calm state. Suddenly I felt all the trouble we had taken coming all this way had been worth it.

As the days went by, we started to become more bonded as a group and began feeling even for those that had irritated us no end in the beginning! Like Vijay, for instance, who had an annoying habit of nibbling snacks all the time. However, Michael never commented or showed any impatience and his compassion and serenity went a long way in helping us to realize how far we had to go, inspite of our spiritual background. It made us see how narrowly we were boxed in our small judgemental minds, which were constantly evaluating things and people: accepting some, rejecting most. We thus naturally imbibed one of the most important lessons in life: "Accept people as they are!" We began to understand that these things, which appear so simple, are actually "*sutras*", secrets of a well-lived life.

When it was time to leave, we all got up and greeted each other, as we had begun, by saying, "I belong to you." And oh, how different it felt this time! Indeed, we actually felt that we had come to belong to each other and that in these six days there had grown a beautiful and touching bond between people who had begun as strangers to each other. Namrita and I looked at each other and realized that something had shifted within us too, we had become lighter, freer from within. It felt as though we had taken a new birth. We had heard about the "born again experience", but till then those had been just words. But now we felt that we had become children again at heart, free and loving. We were standing on the railway platform; there were ten minutes for the train to arrive. Usually, the waiting would have made us restless, but this time it did not matter. And then there was the signal: the train had arrived — metaphorically, to take us on the journey towards a new beginning!

We went back to Auroville, but the memories of The Art of Living Basic Course remained with us and we continued practising the techniques we had learnt. I noticed a significant change in myself. I was not the same person. Suddenly life around me had become much more vibrant. I wondered whether this was a temporary euphoric state. I wanted to see it all. And persistently, one thought kept nagging me: "Who is Sri Sri? Till then I had only heard about him, as he had not been in Bangalore when we had taken our Basic Course. Who was this man, I caught myself wondering, who had devised this incredibly beautiful and powerful Course? I had to see him. Perhaps this curiosity drew me to call up the

Bangalore *ashram*. I was told about the Advanced Course and I signed up for it right away. Namrita chose to stay back.

I went back to Bangalore and drove straight to the *ashram*, which is situated on the Kanakapura road, about twelve miles from the city. "An *ashram* is a place where one comes to rest: *a-shram*, to come home and let go of all your botheration and worries," says Sri Sri. The human mind is such that one instinctively dislikes changing one's surroundings, getting out of the routine, one's habits, known atmosphere and being thrown into a new environment. I felt apprehensive as this *ashram* neared.

The atmosphere at this *ashram* did not reflect the "spirituality" I was used to. People here smiled and laughed. A mood of celebration permeated the place. The hills, greenery, and the lake situated at the other end of the compound — everything was so beautiful. The chirping of birds and insects in the stillness of an autumn evening imbued the place with a magical ambience. In the *ashram* everyone is required to do two hours of *seva* (service) — be it chopping vegetables, translating, transcribing books and speeches, gardening, cleaning the floor, etc. Though groups of people were engaged in various such activities, there was laughter and gaiety everywhere, contrary to my concept of spiritual and religious places as being quiet and serious. A sense of celebration crept into me too. I went around asking what I could do. As I was one of the few westerners there, they gave me some "light work": pruning a bush and watering a few pots.

As I began to do it, I had a burst of enthusiasm. I wanted to do this little job perfectly. Perhaps this is what Sri Sri meant by living in the moment and really enjoying it.

I had the privilege of doing my first Advanced Course with Rajshree and Philip. Rajshree was a thin and intense Indian American, originally a Gujarati. She was a patient, soft-spoken and compassionate teacher, but one could often feel the fire within. We owe her the solid grounding she gave us in the techniques, which we have practised ever since. She was also, like all the senior teachers, totally, entirely and wholeheartedly devoted to Sri Sri. If Rajshree was all fire, Philip was the soft and rounded face of their partnership. Always smiling, ever helpful, perpetually dressed in white kurta and pyjamas, his hair (which was long and black in those times) carefully combed back, Philip was a professional American musician, who had met Guru*ji* by chance and stayed with him. He seemed to us to be the perfect natural teacher, one who had arrived there effortlessly, never putting himself forward, never raising his voice. He would always be the first one to arise in the morning, and we would awake to the melodious sound of his flute. By the time we reached the hall, sleepy and bleary-eyed, he would already be seated there with his eyes closed, looking serene and rested, although he would probably not have slept more than a few hours at night. In fact, it is through Philip that we understood the concept of *seva*, selfless work. Most of Guru*ji*'s teachers never count their time and energy and do not give a thought to a skipped meal or a sleepless night in the service of the Guru. It is a great concept and the key to forgetting oneself.

In fact, it was their sense of commitment, coupled with their humility, which moved me most. I started comparing my editor at *Le Figaro* with them. If only my editor was half as considerate and patient as these people, I could do so much more. Hey! that was an idea, why didn't they teach these techniques to corporate people and journalists? I would convey this to Sri Sri when I meet him, I decided. I thought I was giving him a new idea. I was sure that this was what the world really needed today — an atmosphere of ease, and a sense of celebration, of not losing the commitment, of gaining perfection without stress. I quickly took a pad from my pocket to make some notes sitting under the bush. Then I remembered the instruction to do everything hundred per cent! Realizing I had gotten carried away from the task at hand, I put away my notepad and got back to my shears. My Advanced Course had begun!

As part of the course, we maintained a few days of silence. In the words of Sri Sri Ravi Shankar, "The practice of silence has been known throughout the ages, in many different traditions and cultures, as a great tool for enhancing self-discovery. Maintaining silence, even for just a few days, can have remarkable effects on the system, reviving energy and enthusiasm and providing deep rest for the mind and body." I had done the *Vipassana* course also, but this silence was different. Though I had thoroughly enjoyed *Vipassana*, this revealed to me a new dimension. I realized that silence and joy could go hand in hand and that being in silence need not be too serious or make you morose.

Meditation was another component of the course. Even though I had learnt meditation, Sri Sri's opening sentence, "Meditation is not concentration, it is de-concentration" made me sit-up. This was the introduction to Sri Sri's unique Hollow and Empty Meditation. Philip developed further: "We gain so much from our efforts in life, yet there are some things that effort cannot accomplish. Meditating is the delicate art of doing nothing — letting go of everything and being who you are. It allows the conscious mind to settle deeply into itself; and when the mind settles down, it lets go of all tension and stress and centres itself in the present moment. Regular practice of meditation, once or twice a day can totally transform the quality of your life," he concluded.

On the first evening, we attended, as every night in the *ashram*, a *satsang*, an assembly where everybody sings hymns to the Divine in His different manifestations. *Satsang* was an integral part of the Advanced Course. "The whole day you make efforts, concentrate, use your mind, strive, Rajshree had told us at the end of our session, but during *satsang*, you let go of everything and just be in the togetherness of your hearts." When we entered the meditation hall, Sri Sri Ravi Shankar who had just come back from a trip abroad, was already seated on the dais, eyes closed, in deep meditation. At first, I cannot say that I felt a tremendous revelation in his presence, but remembered Sri Aurobindo's words: "Even if the Divine were to manifest Himself in front of you in His full glory, you would not recognize Him." After some time, thus, I did begin to feel a glow in my heart: something was happening there, a presence, an acknowledgment. By then, the *satsang* was in full swing. I had never attended one before in my entire life and do not care much for singing. But suddenly, it seemed to me as if I recognized these marvellous hymns sung in a foreign tongue, by people from a different culture and background as mine: these were my people, these were my songs, which I had hummed before, though I didn't know where and how! All my fellow course participants were glowing, all had a smile on their faces, some were even in ecstasy, eyes closed, bodies swinging, hands clapping; others had gone into quiet and intense meditation, immobile and relaxed. Sri Sri's eyes were still closed, but there exuded from him such an intense atmosphere of concentrated silence, of deep meditation, of emotionless bliss, that it carried us all away on cloudless skies. As I was gazing at him, he suddenly opened his eyes and looked straight at me, piercing my heart with an emotion I could not fathom. Once again the question sprang up in me: Who was this man?

As after every *satsang*, wherever he is in the world, Sri Sri always answers questions from the participants. I was surprised at the manner in which he tackled the most difficult questions — profound ideas expressed in a few simple words almost making me believe that there was nothing to it! His answers were spontaneous and laced with wit. It seemed he didn't need to think to answer and of course nothing could take his smile away. I noted down some of the points addressed that night:

Q: What happens after death?
Sri Sri: Let there be some suspense! I can assure you, you are not going to miss it. That's for sure!!!
Q: How can one improve patience?
Sri Sri: I will tell you that next year.
Q: How do I improve my memory?
To this question, Sri Sri remained silent for a while, dwelt on other answers, and then came back to that person, saying, "What was your question?"
Q: Do you love everyone equally?
Sri Sri: No, I love everyone uniquely!
Q: Why is it that you have so many followers?
Sri Sri: I don't turn my back on anyone, so how can I have followers?
Q: I'm an interior decorator...
Sri Sri: Oh, we do the same job!
Q: Do you ever get angry?
Sri Sri: I can, but it's very expensive. Make your smile cheap and anger expensive! He laughed and then burst into the *bhajan* which usually concludes *satsangs*: "*Jai, Jai Radhe...*"

The Advanced Course is also all about bonding: by the end you discover how close you can feel to people whom you would have totally ignored in the outside world; how men and women are all wonderful, deep inside, in their essence. Finally, you are made to realize that the art of living well is really all about letting go, dropping your expectations and your hang-ups and realizing how Sri Sri takes you step by step, like a mother leads her child by the hand, from tensions to release, from ego to joy, from darkness to light. By themselves, *seva,* meditation, *satsang* were simple concepts to follow and understand. But their combination as was delivered in the Advanced Course — was the most profound experience I had had till then. Something had shifted! And I was not alone. The shining faces of my co-participants all had a story to tell, I am sure. Here everybody was treated the same. Unlike in many places, there was no VIP treatment for anybody. Talking of Sri Sri, I have to admit that though I was so enamoured of his techniques, I still dissociated them from him and there was no question of surrendering myself to him: I had never bowed to anybody in my life and I was not going to start now. Still, the man fascinated me, his look during *satsang* had pierced my soul and I would observe him from the corner of my eye, peeping out sometimes during the processes he would lead. And when he would cap the Hollow and Empty Meditation with his Sanskrit chanting of *slokas*, always ending with "*Om Shanti, Om Shanti, Om Shanti*", my heart would leap up and something in me would melt beyond redemption.

My desire to meet Sri Sri got fulfilled on the last day of the course. So simple and unpretentious, he asked me about my life, what I did, where I was. He did not try to pressurize me to come back or to become an Art of Living disciple. Yet, his presence conveyed so much love that when I came out, I felt "melted" inside me. When my wife saw me come back to Auroville, radiant and glowing, happy and at peace, something in her also changed and whatever resistance she still had vanished. As for me, I could describe my experience in three words: "It was **fantastic**". We both had work commitments — she had a small children's cloth factory, I was working with *Le Figaro* — but we decided to go back together as soon as possible for another Advanced Course. At the beginning of 1995, we reached the *ashram* again: the smiling faces had become more familiar and Guru*ji* greeted us with a radiant *"Jai Gurudev"*, as if he had always known we would return so fast. Yet again, we had a wonderful course, a unique bonding together and with others. Namrita learnt all these new techniques which I had experienced two months earlier and enjoyed them so much that we decided to return for the next Advanced Course too. In fact, we kept coming back course after course, year after year — we must have done twelve Advanced Courses in four years. Slowly, we too started letting go of some of our resistances towards the guru, experiencing inside us the melting and the sweetness, the gratitude and the love, that all disciples throughout the ages have felt towards their Masters. He made it so easy for us too, never putting pressure on both of us, always saying, "this too is your home", knowing fully well that we were disciples of Sri Aurobindo and the Mother and that Auroville was our base.

On my part, my mind still buzzed with questions: Who was this man? Where had he come from? What was our relationship to be with him? And was not bowing down to him letting go of our capacity to reason and choose, to analyse and discriminate? Was it not surrendering our free will?

CHAPTER TWO

GLIMPSES OF
CHILDHOOD

Stretching sound is music,
Stretching movement is dance,
Stretching the smile is laughter,
Stretching the mind is meditation,
Stretching life is celebration,
Stretching the devotee is GOD,
Stretching feeling is ecstasy,
Stretching emptiness is bliss.

*T*HE MORE YOU APPRECIATE A PERSON, THE MORE YOU want to know about him. Who then is the real Sri Sri behind the empty words of a biography? There is very little that is known of him and he himself, like many yogis, is not very forthcoming about it. One day I ventured to directly ask Guru*ji* myself: "What did you want to be when you were growing up?" "I was a child, I am a child, when did I grow up?" he answered with a twinkle in his eyes. Though I was pleased by his answer, I was not satisfied. It didn't help quench my journalistic curiosity. I felt he had just avoided the question. This is the problem with eastern mystics, I thought, they don't like to talk much about themselves. Perhaps they think this displays humility. These Indians, I concluded, never gave enough importance to history or biography. I didn't understand the logic in such humility.

I wanted to know more. This drew me to enquire from Sri Sri's father, aunt, his sister Bhanu and some of his old associates, friends and classmates. When I asked them about Sri Sri, their eyes would light up and a smile would appear on their faces. They would go on with their stories as though transported back in time. Piecing them all together, this is what I learnt.

Sri Sri Ravi Shankar was born on 13 May 1956 in Papanasam, a village in south India. Sri Sri's father, R S V Ratnam, (referred to as *Pitaji*) was western educated and of modern and reformist thinking. His mother, Visalakshi (referred to as *Amma*), however, hailed from a traditional orthodox Brahmin family. There is a spiritual meaning to his name as he came into the world on Shankara Jayanti, the birth anniversary of Adi Shankara, the great Indian reformer. He was thus named on the eleventh day of his birth, which was Ramanuja Jayanti, the day Ramanuja (another important theologian and Hindu philosopher) was born. And as his native village was famous for its Shiva and Vishnu temples, he was named by his parents "Ravi Shankar". It is only recently that "Ravi" and "Shankar" have been clubbed together into one word. Someone once asked, why Sri Sri comes twice; he is reported to have twinkled and replied, "Because 108 Sris would make it too long."

Little Ravi Shankar showed devotional powers from a very young age and it soon became apparent that he would become a rare and unusual figure.I had heard from various sources that Sri Sri could recite the *Bhagavad*

Gita at a very young age. It seems, when Sri Sri was four, his parents took him to Thangamma, a Sanskrit teacher. She was a Gandhian and would conduct Sanskrit classes and *satsangs* everyday. People from all religious backgrounds would come and learn with her. It is said when the teacher started the first line *"Parthaaya Pratibodhitaam"* and waited for little Ravi Shankar to repeat it and he chanted *"Bhagavataam Narayanena Swayum"* completing the verse! The teacher was astounded that a child could recite from the ancient sacred text when he couldn't read and that too without being taught! When he was taken to the nearby school, to begin his academic career, his teachers recognized his extraordinary intelligence, and he was given two double promotions! By the time he was seventeen, he had a fair amount of knowledge of Vedic literature, had completed his traditional studies and secured a Bachelor's degree in modern science!

When young Ravi Shankar expressed an interest in learning Sanskrit, his parents arranged for classes with Pandit Sudakar Chaturvedi. The Pandit was Mahatma Gandhi's Sanskrit teacher as well as his secretary for south India. Gandhi*ji* used to call him "Bangalori". Young Sri Sri was the Pandit's first pupil since the Mahatma. There is an interesting story behind this fact. During Partition, the Mahatma was deeply pained. He was losing faith in all his close aides. When the news of Hindus and Muslims fighting with each other reached him, he refused to believe it. To get a first-hand account, he sent Pandit Chaturvedi to Lahore. Upon reaching there, Bangalori saw that it was the Hindus who were being tortured and killed by the Muslims; he himself was attacked, stripped, beaten, stabbed several times and buried up to the neck in a sand pit. He was saved in the nick of time by an army officer. When he narrated the scene, which was worse than a civil war to Gandhi*ji*, the Mahatma refused to believe him, saying that he was reporting all these things because he was a Hindu himself. Bangalori was deeply hurt that Gandhi*ji* had lost faith in him also. Upset and annoyed he returned to Bangalore. Three days later the Mahatma was assassinated. Pandit Chaturvedi used to share this story with everyone, ending with regret that he felt he had deserted the Mahatma in his last days. In Bangalore, he wrote books and gave talks in the Arya Samaj. He did not formally teach anyone till young Ravi Shankar came along.

Once, when he was five years old, an aged Pandit, Samba Dixit, visited Guru*ji*'s house. Dixit displayed various deities and asked the lad to choose one of them. Ravi Shankar chose a Shiva *lingam* made of emerald and a silver serpent. Dixit was impressed and disclosed that the *lingam* originally belonged to the family of Muthuswami Dikshitar — a renowned saint and singer of south India who lived over three hundred years ago. He interpreted it as a sign that young Ravi Shankar would grow up to be an upholder of truth and righteousness (*dharma*).

As a young child, Ravi Shankar was a keen observer and rebellious by nature. He could not accept injustice in any form. When he was around nine years old, he had gone to his maternal grandmother's place for the summer vacations. Here he came across the practice of untouchability for the first time. Bangalore being a cosmopolitan city, he had not been exposed to it there. He was very fond of cows and calves and the man who would take care of them was a *harijan* named Swaminathan. He observed that Swaminathan was not allowed to enter his home and even had to have his food outside the house after everyone had eaten. Young Sri Sri was not allowed to touch him and if he did, he was punished and promptly made to take a bath. Swaminathan was happy the way he was, but not young Ravi Shankar. This was unacceptable. He questioned his grandmother, "Why do you treat him so?" Pat came the reply, " He is an untouchable." In response, Sri Sri would quote from the *Bhagavad Gita* "*Ishvaro Sarvabhutanam ...*" meaning, God lives in every heart, in every human being. It fell on deaf ears. But the rebel in him would not be quiet and he would touch Swaminathan and then touch his grandmother and then all her clothes, which she would have hung in the house. She would not let anyone, not even her family members touch her clothes and Sri Sri would go and pull all of them down! He would also share his food with Swaminathan's children. One day he went away on Swaminathan's bicycle to his house. This created such a storm in the family, that the very next day his mother had to take him back to Bangalore.

Sri Sri was very attached to his grandmother even though he did not agree with her on the topic of untouchability. And when he discovered that people die after they grow old, he became very anxious and was afraid to lose her. He used to sleep with her and sit at night watching her breathing, because he connected breath with life. "Every time I felt she was not breathing," he recalls today, "I would wake her up and as long as she was snoring — which she did loudly — I was happy." It is at this time that he often saw dreams that if he touched her when she died, she would come alive. But when she did die, he did not touch her "as by that time I had understood that there is no death and was afraid that if I touched her she would indeed come alive and that all my waiting and watching would have to be resumed!" Sri Sri also could not tolerate others' pain and suffering. In his house, there was a young servant girl in her teens who would do all the household chores like cleaning the house and vessels, mopping the floor, washing the clothes etc. While his sister had fun, the servant had to do all the jobs. They both were of the same age. This was a cause of sorrow to him, and he had many fights on this issue at home.

Nevertheless, little Ravi Shankar was also a child who loved to play pranks. One day, when his father opened his briefcase in the midst of official discussions, he found it full of toys, instead of official documents. All his colleagues had a hearty laugh at his expense. When in the evening, he met his son and emptied the briefcase of all the toys, Sri Sri simply laughed and pointed at the piles of papers arranged neatly along with his other toys! *Pitaji* burst into laughter on seeing his lovely laughing face.

Eager to know more about Sri Sri's childhood, I approached Bhanu, Sri Sri's sister. My first impression of her was of beauty and laughter. When I asked her how it felt to be Sri Sri's sister, she just giggled in her characteristic way. Then she said, "I always wanted to be where my brother was. I was not interested in hanging out with my friends. In fact, my parents had to seek special permission so that I could accompany my brother on his class trip!" I asked, "Didn't you ever fight with each other?" She said, "Whenever I would do something that would displease him, instead of fighting or yelling, he would just go and sit calmly in a corner with his eyes closed. I would go near him and try to get him to speak, but nothing would disturb him. He would just smile!" Sri Sri's paternal aunt says, "Sri Sri would spend a lot of time observing the rituals in churches, mosques and temples. Whatever he learnt or noticed, he would share it with Bhanu."

"There was a woman in my life, who loved me more than herself," says Sri Sri. Guru*ji*'s mother seems to be the woman who had the biggest impact on his life. The story of her birth and death is as interesting and as full of mystery as his life. Her parents, while on a pilgrimage to Kashi, a city considered the holiest in India prayed for a child at a temple of the Mother Divine. About ten months later, a child was born. She was named Visalakshi, after the same temple Goddess to whom the parents had prayed. *Amma* grew up in a simple orthodox south Indian family surrounded by a host of relatives. She had an aunt called Savithri who used to teach her and her sisters singing and playing the veena at home. As a young girl she picked up both these fine arts very well. Her grasping power was very good and she would memorize any new *ragas* taught to her very quickly. She studied in the Government High School for Girls in Papanasam till SSC (Senior School Certificate) and Sanskrit was one of the languages that she was very proficient in. She got married to RSV Ratnam in 1955.

After marriage, she moved to Bangalore. She was always fond of feeding people and soon the title *Annapoorneshwari* (Goddess of food) got added to her name and till the very end she continued this tradition. Today it is perpetuated by her daughter. Both devotees and teachers had great respect and affection for her. This is how Sri Sri reminisces about her today: "When I was a child, some astrologer told my mother, 'Your son was born on Shankar Jayanti day and he is going to leave you, he will become an ascetic.' This made her anxious, but I reassured her that I would not leave her. However, all her relatives would berate her, 'What has happened to your son? He talks philosophy, he does not behave like a normal person... You better find him a job and get him married quickly," they would advise. Then, once again she would feel a little confused for a couple of days, until *Pitaji* would console her saying, 'Don't worry, he has very fine stars, he will turn out well, don't worry.' Other people would tell her, 'Don't allow your son to do so much *puja*, he may go mad and crazy. He will not study properly.' So every time I would sit for meditation, she would hurry me up saying, 'Not yet over? You are taking too long. Come on. Study.' Sometimes she would ask me to do *Sandhyavandana* instead of *puja*. I would go and do it but it would take me one-and-a-half hours while my cousins would finish the same in ten minutes! When I would somehow escape the sports class now and then, come home and do something else, she would scold, 'Why did you come so early, go and play football.' But l would look at my feet and I would think: these feet cannot kick anybody, let alone the ball and I would refuse to go."

Sri Sri also recollects that sometimes she would hide all his *puja* items. He would come back from school, start crying and say that he wouldn't eat till all those things were given back to him. He also says today that he did all his degrees to please his mother and on her compulsion, he even went for an interview with a bank. But as it turned out, he interviewed them instead of the other way around! They asked him what he was doing. When they found out that he taught meditation they got so interested, they wanted to know more, and he sat and gave them a nice talk! He was selected and was given the to-and-fro fare to Delhi. However, he was not interested in taking up the job, so he spent one or two days in Rishikesh and returned to Bangalore. Knowing that *Amma* did not want him to go far away from her, he would tease her about taking up a job in the Merchant Navy, from where he kept getting letters and job offers. He comments today, "*Amma* didn't wish me to go that far. But she definitely wanted me to take up a job in one of the banks." When asked if his mother would ever scold him, Sri Sri smiles and says that she did so when she found him returning from trips with an empty suitcase. He enjoyed sharing all that he had — money, clothes, everything — with others!

CHAPTER THREE

THE CELEBRATION
THAT IS SILENCE

Give me not thirst, if you cannot give me water.

Give me not hunger, if you cannot give me food.

Give me not joy, if you cannot share.

Give me not skills, if I cannot put them to good use.

Give me not intelligence, if I cannot perceive beyond it.

Give me not love, if I cannot serve.

Give me not desires, if they do not lead me to you.

Give me not a path, if it does not take me home.

Give me not prayers, if you will not hear them.

*H*AVE YOU EVER BEEN IN A RELIGIOUS FESTIVAL IN INDIA? Celebrations here are frenzied. In that chaos, somehow I procured an invitation to attend the *Navaratri* celebrations at the Bangalore *ashram*. It is a celebration of silence amidst pandemonium. *Navaratri* honours the nine aspects of Mother Divine. The atmosphere was simply electrifying. In spite of the huge crowds, there was this incredible energy and serenity which I have never felt before. After the festivities, we were sitting in a group with Bhanu. She said, "This is the first *Navaratri* without *Amma*." I suddenly realized it had been one year since she passed away. Bhanu continued sharing about *Amma*'s last days. She said, "I found her behaviour 'odd'. It was strange that a strong-willed woman like her, who had always been in charge of everything seemed to be turning over all responsibility. Maybe she was preparing me to take care of the house, children and family. However, she performed all the *Yagnas* fully." The day after *Navaratri*, she was hospitalized.

When *Amma* breathed her last, Sri Sri was at Varanasi. There were eight thousand people whom he had to address the very day he lost the person dearest to him. I was with him that day and saw the depth of his silence, serenity and patience in attending to everybody in those trying moments. Yet the smile did not fade away. To the devotees who were with Guru*ji* at that time, and knew his attachment to *Amma*, it was a lesson in equanimity. Rajshree Patel reminisces, "I always knew he loved his mother very dearly, but I did not realize the depth of his love until after she had passed away. At the International Millennium Course in Italy, a month or so after the death of his mother, I discovered yet another dimension to Sri Sri. On the one hand everyone is the same to him, his love is impersonal and yet, I was learning, it was deeply personal. We were sitting in an assembly of fifteen hundred to two thousand people. Someone in the front row was holding a magazine with *Amma*'s photo on it. Sri Sri with a certain depth in his voice was speaking of gratitude in life. Giving a brief pause he said, 'There was a woman in my life, who loved me more than herself.' Everybody sat up. He gestured to the magazine and added, 'She was my mother.' A tear of deep love and gratitude for her rolled down his face and I suddenly felt a total connectedness to him and I started crying uncontrollably.

And for the first time in all the years that I knew him, I saw the deepest personal love possible, free of attachment and demands yet full of gratitude."

"People ask me, who is Guru*ji* to you ? My answer is simple: he is both my son and my master," says R S V Ratnam, Guru*ji*'s father. *Pitaji* hails from a prominent family that has been responsible for many path-breaking developmental activities in the state of Karnataka. He is engaged in research on the modern applications of the ancient Vedic wisdom. He also has the ability to weave lifeless words into uplifting stories from the Puranas. Though seventy-seven years of age, he is a tireless worker for social causes and guides several projects for the rehabilitation and emancipation of rural women. It is through him that we got to know more about Sri Sri's childhood. He recounts an interesting incident: "In olden days, big households in rural areas of south India had heavy cradles, in which the child and the mother could swing and sleep. It was also thought to be a status symbol. My wife's ancestors being the leaders of the village had built a long single-storeyed house with its front door facing the temple street. The broad corridor-cum-hall of the house had one such big wooden cradle tied by four heavy iron chains, to a solid wooden beam above. One day, as I entered the house and approached the cradle, my wife saw me and immediately got up from the cradle to receive me. That was the fatal moment, when with the child still in it, suddenly all the iron chains holding the cradle snapped and it fell to the ground with a loud noise.

When she heard the sound of the crash, the thought of losing the baby was too much for my wife and she fainted. I had to swiftly step forward to hold her in my arms, as I looked simultaneously at the cradle, expecting to see a seriously hurt child under the heavy chains. But, lo! something beyond my comprehension was happening and my head, filled as it was with fear, refused to believe what my eyes were seeing! Was it true or was I dreaming? There, inside the damaged cradle was the child playfully smiling, while all the heavy chains, instead of falling inside the cradle, had fallen out, defying all laws. My sister-in-law who was nearby, ran to the cradle, picked up the child, and cried out in relief, 'The boy is safe, the boy is safe.' It took some time for my wife to regain consciousness and composure, but when the smiling infant was placed in her arms, though a little dazed, she held the baby to her bosom, and began to laugh and cry at the same time. Later, with trembling hands and tearful eyes, she handed the baby to me, with the words, "God has saved our son.' "

Pitaji adds: "When Guru*ji* was around two years old, his mother, while she had work to do, would often make him sit in the corridor of the house facing the garden and point out the birds and other small creatures, which sing and sway with the wind and sun. The young child, with wide-eyed interest would laugh and clap his hands in glee till he was called back. One day while his mother was preparing his food, she was called out and before going, she made him sit at a distance from the stove and said,

'Don't go near the stove, the heat will hurt you.' When she came back after a while, she found him still sitting calmly watching with interest, the burning stove and boiling water. He had made no attempt to move and looked up at her with his laughing eyes. It was indeed a joy to observe the child's total faith in his mother and her total confidence in him. This totality of faith, confidence and love blossomed in later years and covered everybody around him."

"Eighteen months after his birth," continues *Pitaji*, "his sister Bhanu came into this world, a fair, restless infant, fond of sweets, toys and tales, a counterpoint to her brother who was calm, composed and confident. I used to say that she was the other side of the coin. When he was shown his younger sister, he bent forward and touched her head and then in childlike innocence asked us, 'From where did she come?' For want of a better answer, his mother replied, 'The doctor gave her to us.' 'Will she be taken away?' was his next question. Jokingly I said, 'Will you give her away, if the doctor asks you to?' 'No,' was his emphatic reply. 'I will not give her away. She belongs to us.' This feeling of protective love for his sister came to the fore often. In fact, respect for elders, love to youngsters, focus on the jobs at hand and a feeling of belongingness formed the basis of his actions and activities even while he was young. As he grew, these qualities expanded to cover more and more people and today every one of us realize that he is an apostle of love and confidence.

"Even as a youngster, Gurudev was more concerned about other's welfare. I recollect the day when my aged mother took him for the first time to the nearby grocer. When they left home, he grasped her hand tightly and she assumed that it was for his security. But she was very surprised and amused when the young fellow cautioned her saying, 'Grandma! Be careful. Hold my hand so that you do not fall.' His voice had a ring of maturity quite unconnected to his tender age."

Pitaji also remembers that, "many saints and seers visited their home and when very young, the Shankaracharyas (Senior pontiffs) of south India's most respected and revered *matths* — Sringeri and Kanchi — recognized the divine spark in the young child and blessed him. One day, His Holiness Shri Shankaracharya of Shivganga visited our house and accepted *puja* and offerings. During the celebrations, *Amma* brought the child out and laid him at his feet. The Acharya saw the lovely face of the baby and noticed some special marks on his back. His eyes shone with joy when he said, 'Your child is Divine. You are lucky and blessed to be his parents,' and folded his hands in respect to young Sri Sri. Once, we visited a Ganesh temple and the big elephant head of the Divinity fascinated him. 'Why does he have such a big head?' was his query and I replied, 'Because he has storage of great knowledge in it.' 'So people with big heads have more knowledge, is it?' was his next question. I was rather taken aback by this innocent twist in logic, but managed to answer, 'It is not quite like that. Ganesh has a big head, but if we pray to him, He will put much knowledge into our small heads too.' "

Guru*ji*'s father recollects that "beggars presented a mystery to my son. 'Why are they begging?' he would ask his mother. 'Because they are poor,' my wife would reply. 'But why are they poor?' Being stuck for an answer, she would gently divert him to me. After a vain search for a satisfactory answer, I was forced to say, 'God made them poor,' since I did not wish to burden the young mind with the harsh karmic theory. But his answer was stunning. He calmly said, 'Then I will ask God, not to make beggars.' What a mature resolve from a tender heart!

"Gurudev was a keen observer and noted all the procedures of *puja* that the temple priest performed and he would try to emulate them at home. Even when he was only three years old, he had learnt a few mantras. He would often close his eyes and repeat them. When once I asked him what he wanted from the Lord, he promptly said, 'I want everyone to be happy. I don't like people quarrelling.' Tolerance and joy were the basis of the young master's attitudes. When we admitted him into a nursery school next to our home in Bangalore, he became the favourite of both the teacher and the tiny tots. They used to crowd around him and he would tell them the stories he had heard from me. One day, he went to the school and was back home shortly, followed by all the boys and girls of his class. To his surprised mother, he calmly said, 'The teacher has gone home for some work, and I brought the students home, for some play. Can you please give them something to eat?' On her return to the school the poor teacher was shocked to find the whole class empty. She ran to our house and found them enraptured by his stories. Later when she asked him, why he had taken them all home, he simply replied, 'There is so much noise outside, and we all wanted to eat something,' forgetting the fact that the children produced more noise inside than what was noticed outside! When Ravi Shankar was four years of age and his sister two, both would chant and pray, much to the amazement of the people around. When asked what it was that they prayed for, pat came the reply — 'for everyone to be happy!' "

CHAPTER FOUR

DAYS WITH
MAHARISHI

Celebrate while you are alone and celebrate
when you are with people.
Celebrate silence and celebrate noise.
Celebrate life and celebrate death.

*I*N SRI SRI, YOU CAN FIND A BEAUTIFUL BLEND OF VEDA and Science. This seed sprouted in him when he came in contact with His Holiness Maharishi Mahesh Yogi, whose Transcendental Meditation (TM) was known the world over. Maharishi was at that time conducting Veda and Science conferences all over India and bringing scientists and Vedic scholars together on the same platform. In those days, Dr. E C George Sudarshan, a renowned professor of physics, former Supreme Court Judge Justice V R Krishna Iyer and the then Chief Justice of India Justice P N Bhagawati, were travelling with Maharishi. Sri Sri took part in one such meeting in Bangalore. Maharishi Mahesh Yogi spotted the young Ravi Shankar and asked him to accompany him on the tour.

Sri Sri went with Maharishi to Rishikesh and spent some time there. When Maharishi Mahesh Yogi used to organize *Sant Sammelans* (congregation of saints), Sri Sri used to be the anchor welcoming the saints and taking care of their hospitality. Though Sri Sri was very young, he was a very good organizer, which Maharishi appreciated. He was thus sent to various places to give talks on the Vedas and science. It is at that time that he started growing a beard, "to look a little mature", he explains," because the people I had to teach meditation to did not take me seriously!" His mother did not necessarily approve. "She wanted me to take it off, because she was not used to it at all. Here, in the south, everybody is clean-shaven, so it took her a little while to get used to it."

Very little is known about Guru*ji*'s time with Maharishi, but from the few words he said, it is obvious that it was a momentous period. Maharishi used to send Sri Sri to represent him at the various *matths* and *ashrams* — including the Ordaining Ceremony of Guru Mai Chidvilasanand by her Guru Baba Muktanand. Sri Sri went to Ganeshpuri (Baba Muktanand's Ashram) with two truckloads of sweets. Baba Muktanand very warmly received him and the group of pandits with him. Later, Maharishi dispatched Sri Sri to different European countries to give talks on Veda and Science. He worked tirelessly to set up the Veda, Science and Ayurveda centres. In 1980, Maharishi wanted Guru*ji* to organize a big *yagna* in Noida, (a place 30 km away from New Delhi) along with a mammoth Vedic conference. It turned out to be a big success and Maharishi was so happy with it, that he made plans for an even bigger *yagna* at Diwali time, which would be performed by six thousand pandits. Soon after, Sri Sri left with Maharishi for Switzerland and the *yagna s* preparation was left to others in the organization. Recalls Guru*ji* today, "Maharishi had his own style of celebrating and did everything with a lot of pomp and show. For this particular ceremony, he wanted everything to be in yellow as far as the eye could see, as this was the colour of Goddess Laxmi. So all the sweets were to be yellow, decorations in yellow and gold coins from different countries were brought for this *yagna...*" But when Sri Sri returned with Maharishi from Switzerland with three thousand Westerners who were to witness the *yagna*, he realized that there were serious lapses in organizing the event. Many of the pandits who had been recruited were not really pandits. But it was too late: as soon as the *puja* was over, there was a riot, with all the pandits rushing for the sweets! The foreigners who were there, were baffled with what was happening. "Just to make them comfortable, recalls Guru*ji*,they were told it was a game, it was the tradition!"

Maharishi asked Sri Sri to look into the reasons for the failure of the *yagna* and the chaos that followed. Those responsible knew that Sri Sri, through his insight and intuition, would quickly find out that kickbacks had been received for recruiting people who were not really pandits, and that they would be caught. Since many of the "fake" pandits were from the state of Bihar, they spread a rumour that Sri Sri did not like Biharis. Several people cautioned Sri Sri not to go there as they anticipated big trouble, but he still proceeded to Noida to meet the pandits. Waiting for him, there were around a thousand Biharis with black flags, burning torches and shouting slogans against him and threatening to set fire to him and his car. He told the leader that they could do what they liked to him, but they should give him half an hour to talk to them. Having secured this reprieve, he told them that he had nothing against Biharis, but that when *yagnas* are not performed properly, and the chanting of the *mantras* is not done correctly, it can cause harm to the country and even the people who perform the *yagnas*. Then he said that they would be tested and that anybody who was not good at chanting *mantras* would be put to do some other work: carpentry, masonry, labour, etc. Thus Guru*ji* in his charismatic manner changed everything around and settled the matter.

Inevitably this created jealousy in the organization and the fact that many worldly men and saints praised Guru*ji* did not help either. Ramnath Goenka, the baron of the *Indian Express* paper, for instance, who used to often meet Maharishi, called Sri Sri "a beacon of light". When Maharishi took the young Ravi Shankar to Ananda Mai Ma in Brindavan, she said to Maharishi, "Ah, you have brought me the Ganges," indicating that he was going to purify the world. A famous astrologer of Delhi, Gyanchand Shastri, who had written more than two hundred books, dedicated his book on "Yoga Sutras" to Sri Sri. Another time, Guru*ji* met Kotiswamy in Pollachi, Tamil Nadu, reputed to be four hundred years old and asked him for some knowledge. Kotiswamy looked at him and said, "When Shiva himself asks for knowledge, what can I give him?" People then started to whisper in Maharishi's ear that Guru*ji* was trying to usurp his place. Guru*ji* then thought about leaving, but was reluctant to do so because at that time many good persons were already deserting Maharishi for one reason or the other. Besides, he had a lot of respect for Maharishi, who, he says today, "had a lion-like personality, transformed the world and brought spirituality to the West. He had good energy, was humorous, and was still as a rock when he meditated. He never listened to gossipers and did not like people to complain. If anybody started to complain about someone, he would show them the door." Maharishi, on his part, was always very proud of Guru*ji* and used to say, "The sun (Ravi) rises and there will be light everywhere."

CHAPTER FIVE

THE WAY IT
ALL BEGAN

Knowledge is a burden if it robs you of
   innocence;
Knowledge is a burden if it makes you feel
   you are special;
Knowledge is a burden if it gives you an idea
   that you are wise;
Knowledge is a burden, if it does not bring
   you joy;
Knowledge is a burden, if it does not set
   you free.

*I*N 1980, MAHARISHI ONCE MORE SENT SRI SRI TO ASSIST another *yagna* and asked him to meditate there, so as to ensure the success of the ceremony. Guru*ji* recalls that he used to sit and meditate from 8 in the morning to 4 o'clock in the evening, with only a half-hour break in between. He did this for forty days. Then he would come back in the evenings, attend to all the lectures and work of Maharishi till 3 in the morning and again be back at the *yagna* at 6 a.m. This went on for six months and made his health fragile, specially as he could not eat in Noida because of the polluted atmosphere there.

Maharishi wanted to start Vedic schools all over India, so he sent Sri Sri to Bangalore for a rest and to start the Ved Vigyan Vidya Peeth. Two hundred children for this school were recruited from Karnataka by *Pitaji*. This was to be an independent setup as Maharishi did not want to be dependent on the Government's grants and land to start these schools. A trust was set up with Sri Sri, Justice V R Krishna Iyer, Lakshman Rao, the Mayor of Bangalore and Justice P N Bhagawati. As was often done, the TM movement decided to close down the schools in the south and bring all the children to the north in Delhi, but this did not turn out to be feasible as many of the parents did not agree to the move. After two years of their children being in the new system of education, they could now neither go back to the previous setup nor continue in Delhi. This would have resulted in around two hundred court cases. Sri Sri took on the responsibility to house, feed and educate all the children.

At this juncture many from the TM movement came down to Bangalore to persuade Sri Sri to stay with the organization, which he politely refused. Most people thought that Sri Sri had gone crazy. How could he house, feed and educate so many children without any source of income? But as it happened, just the day the students were to come, somebody came forward and offered their house for the students to stay. Another turned up and offered to look after the arrangements for their food! One after another, miracles happened and Sri Sri managed effortlessly to run the school. In fact, he had never wanted to start another organization. Even though he was only twenty-five, he had already witnessed a wide range of life — from helicopters to bullock carts. He had walked to different remote villages, stayed in small huts and nothing could sway him. It is during this period, in early 1982, that he decided to go into ten days of silence. Though he was giving talks and lectures and conducting meditation he felt that there was something more needed to make a difference in people's lives. This innate restlessness gave birth to the Art of Living Course and the *Sudarshan Kriya*. When questioned about this, he is reported to have answered that he knew something was "coming up".

The first course was held in Shimoga, India. It is said that he remained silent throughout the course. At first the participants were baffled, but slowly, they felt he was actually teaching them, communicating knowledge through the sacredness of silence and when he began to speak, many felt that they had already heard what he had to say. It is also in 1982 that he established the Art of Living Foundation, as an educational organization designed to assist all levels of society in achieving their full human potential. For five years, Sri Sri taught the courses himself. 'The *kriyas* used to last from two to three hours, and the courses went on from eight in the morning till eleven at night, with only a small break for lunch at 5 o'clock! "I was very tough, in the ego-busting sessions, for instance," he recalls today.

There are many stories of Sri Sri's early teachings. I will narrate here only a few. Sri Sri was conducting courses in England. He used to meet with the public for one hour a day in the home of Poppat-*bhai*, the owner of a London shoe company. Many healings are reported to have happened there: someone who could not walk started walking, someone who could not talk properly, began delivering fluent speeches and Poppat-*bhai*'s daughter, who was suffering from thyroid problems, became all right after only two meditation sessions with Sri Sri. There was also a young boy, Chetan, whose eyes would water constantly because of some rare disease. Sri Sri told his parents that they should tie a pearl with no hole around his neck. But where were they to find this perfect pearl, they wondered? Lo and behold, when they got home, they discovered a pearl without a hole in their altar. They tied it on him and he got cured. Another time, Sri Sri was staying with Mr Bharadwaj in Southall, London and there was a talk organized for him in a temple. They had just arrived there and only one *bhajan* had been sung, when Sri Sri got up suddenly and said he wanted to go back to the house. Everybody was surprised but nobody argued with the young Master. Upon reaching the house, they found Mrs Bharadwaj lying on the floor in a semi-coma after a severe attack. Sri Sri just put his hand on her head and by the time the ambulance arrived, she was perfectly all right! People began to queue up for fulfilment of this or that desire or healing. There was very little interest in the knowledge. "I didn't want people to become greedy, but to blossom in knowledge," remembers Sri Sri. To this end, he started the teachers training programme.

Once, while in Assisi, Italy, Sri Sri was taking a walk with a few devotees. He suddenly pointed out a nearby hill and suggested that they walk to the top of it. By the time they got there, it was drizzling and there was a pink cloud on the horizon. On top of the hill was an old chapel. In that chapel was a catholic priest who did not speak any English. This chapel was not very popular, because the priest spoke about reincarnation and wanted to make his church into a multicultural place. When the priest saw Sri Sri, he was overwhelmed with joy and asked him to step into his church. He said that he had a vision that Sri Sri would be visiting and that at that time it would be drizzling and there would be a pink cloud in the sky! The priest shared that he had never experienced so much love and peace in his whole life as he felt in that one interaction. Another time in Italy, while walking with a few devotees, Sri Sri suddenly ran towards a bush. Everybody wondered what he was doing. He found a man sitting and praying desperately to be "taken away" by the hand of God. The man was a scuba diver who had had an out-of-body experience while under water, and had tried many things to re-experience it, without success. When he saw Guru*ji*, he was in a state of shock, and started to follow him around. Guru*ji* probably gave him what he wanted, because one day he disappeared as mysteriously as he had appeared.

On his return *Pitaji*'s house in Bangalore became too small to contain Sri Sri's activity in India, Sri Sri inspired *Pitaji* to involve himself in service projects, and soon with *Pitaji*'s help, he started developing an *ashram* on rocky wasteland just on the outskirts of Bangalore.

Pitaji recalls how it all started:

"The very first effort to start the Ved Vigyan Maha Vidya Peeth was on 13th November 1981 in Bangalore city. Why November 13th? Because Sri Sri wanted to prove that there is nothing inauspicious about the number 13! We had 150 students who had to be fed, clothed and educated within the small house of Jayanagar (where the Sri Sri Media Centre now stands). Meanwhile, we were looking for land to establish the *ashram*: it took us four years to get it sanctioned! In April 1985, we got sixty acres of land leased for thirty years and in October we started on that very spot our very first Sanskrit school with twenty students and we also quickly transferred the Vedic school there. By October 1985 we had erected temporary buildings, but still had no water. People said that the area was too rocky to find water, but Sri Sri pointed out a certain place and said we should be able to find it there. We started drilling: hundred feet, no water, two hundred feet, three hundred feet, still no water... The contractor told me it was useless to continue and waste money, but I was sure that if Sri Sri said water was there, it was bound to be. And at 310 feet, water started gushing out!

"Within two years we had more temporary buildings made out of brick and red earth mortar, which housed twenty people, including the cook who stayed in the *ashram*, but there was still no electricity. At that time, Sri Sri was travelling all over India and the west and did not spend more than one-and-half months per year in the *ashram*. Thus, for nearly twelve years, I was then more or less running the place though we could all feel his presence and it was as if he was there all the time, giving us directions. What actually gave us a tremendous boost was the first international conference in 1988 — eighty people attended from all over the world, and it was such a success, that thereafter, it was repeated every two years.

"I was also putting a lot of energy into the school — in the beginning, we used to face opposition from other schools, as we were not charging any fees. Added to this was the fact that we asked the children to chant '*Vande mataram*' and taught them '*Om namah shivaya*', which made some people say that we were a 'communal organization'. But soon, not only hundred per cent of our children passed, but also, it was the Bengali and Christian students who came first in the Bhagavad-Gita competition, which showed that actually we were very secular in spirit. Then there was the Vedic Science Research Institute which we set up. In the beginning, the Government was very sceptical, but quickly we were able to prove that there are more than seventy-one scientific disciplines in the Vedas and now we are recognized by the Government as a serious body."

After the international conference, Sri Sri went with a few Indian and western devotees to meet Kotiswamy. He was a saint who lived in a town twelve kilometres from Pollachi, near Coimbatore, Tamil Nadu and was reputed to be around 450 years old. He passed away recently, in 1998. Kotiswamy used to speak about his experiences of walking with Swami Vivekananda, over hundred years ago! The "oldest" resident, who was ninety-three years old, said that his grandfather had also seen Kotiswamy in the same place! There are records with the municipality of Pollachi. Kotiswamy would sit on the terrace of an old house all the time. There was one servant who watched the door. Apparently, he hadn't ever moved from there for several decades! People would come to see him, put garlands around him or feed him. He had to be fed. As the legend goes, the Swami would eat, but would not defecate. Even in the hot climate of Pollachi, he would wear twenty to thirty robes, one on top of another! Sri Sri requested him to give him some knowledge. Kotiswamy looked at him and said, "When Shiva himself asks for knowledge, what can I give him?"

Rajshree, with whom I spoke about the start of the AOL movement, added, "Sri Sri is so clear in his mind. He is like a mirror. He reflects our true nature. I haven't found anybody with whom I can work with such ease and comfort. At the same time, I cannot cope with his energy. He can go on working for hours without getting tired and his intentions are very powerful. Simultaneously, he is so childlike. While flying once from Bombay to Bangalore with him the first time, he said to me, "You will love Bangalore, it is the garden city, and our *ashram* is so green." I am unable to recall what I was expecting, but the city of gardens had a lot more cement than trees or flowers. The *ashram*, well, it was barren, dry, hilly, rocky and infested with snakes. There were three small buildings and huts, which Sri Sri called "temporary housing". Apparently, there had been an International Conference in 1988 with about sixty to eighty people. Some of the students at the time were housed there and others were in a nearby facility. The buildings were initially erected for the Vedic pandit boys. *Narayana Kutir* was a leaky hut with a small room for meditation and even smaller adjoining bedroom for Sri Sri. *Shakti Kutir*, his current cottage, was just being completed: a small round building with only one room that had a tiny mattress on the floor on one side and a low wooden chair on the other. Until 1994, the cottage was just this, small and simple. Later, two other rooms were added. Regardless of the growth of the Foundation, Sri Sri and his lifestyle have always remained simple and humble. As the organization grew, more and more people wanted to serve and offer donations. I remember when, on a number of different occasions, a very wealthy family or an individual, would offer to build the entire *ashram* with all the modern facilities and luxury. I, who had come from the West, jumped at the idea: no more electricity cuts, no more water shortage, possibilities of having water heaters, air conditioners, etc., but Sri Sri always refused. I never understood why he refused such generous offers, till one day, he explained to me the idea of *Guru Dakshina*. (the skilful way of giving): "This *ashram* will bring peace to all those who come here. It is a blessing and a gift to be able to give comfort and peace in life. One can give money, one can give food, but to give peace of mind is the highest gift of all and everyone should partake in that offering. It is as a family that we will build this home."

Many a time, when we all walked around the *ashram*, he would describe the location of different buildings: "There will be a coliseum, on top of the hill, a kitchen here and the meditation hall there." He described the land and the location of structures with such details that I assumed there was a concrete plan laid out on paper. The plan was laid out; only it was not on paper. In answer to my question about blueprints, he always smiled and stated, "In the big blue sky the prints are fixed." The buildings were constructed, as need for them arose. When the meditation hall was being constructed, at every pillar, within a distance of about eight feet different soil and minerals were being dug up. Geologically this was inexplicable but Sri Sri explained that the ancient *Rishis* used the land for *yagnas* and it was the reason for the variation of soil and minerals within such a short span of space.

So many times as we approached the land, from the car he would say, "Isn't our *ashram* so beautiful, so green?" The only green thing I could see were a few papaya trees. I thought either something is wrong with him or with me. All I noticed were brown rocks and dirt. But today, it is indeed like the Garden of Eden. Our stroll always ended at the top of the hill, where the coliseum (*Sumeru*) stands today. He would look out into space and then down the hill, and tell us: "One day this whole hill will be covered with thousands of people, there will be an amphitheatre for sitting arrangements, I will not even be able to walk because there will be such a crowd and there will be a screen where they will have to project everything." On one level, I knew all that he was saying would be so in the future. On another level I wondered how it would become possible? There were barely eight to ten people coming to *satsang* at the time, the idea of thousands seemed incomprehensible. Unknown to all of us, the platform was being laid for the phenomenal growth of The Art of Living in India. Today, when I look back and remember those *ashram* strolls with Sri Sri, I recall with amazement his quiet yet resolute statement: "Everything is set."

CHAPTER SIX

FROM BEING A STUDENT TO A TEACHER

The Sun rises and celebrates,
The sky embraces and celebrates,
Winds blow and celebrate,
Rivers flow and celebrate,
Birds sing and celebrate,
Peacocks dance and celebrate,
Trees flower and celebrate,
Buds blossom and celebrate,
We smile and serve,
meditate and celebrate.

TIME PASSED BY, BUT MY CURIOSITY NEVER EBBED. BY now we had taken many Advanced Courses, and were in touch with the techniques, and the knowledge. I had seen, during Advanced Courses, how the TTC groups (Teachers' Training Course) had a special bonding, an incredible abundance of energy and laughter. It filled me with admiration, making me nearly envious! Doing the Teachers' Training seemed thus a logical progression into newer horizons. We told Guru*ji* we wanted to do it and he seemed to approve of it — so we went ahead.

The Teachers' Training is very special and only those who have done it, will understand what I am talking about. I have not spoken so far about the great privilege it is to be born an Indian — and I think this is as good an occasion as any. When I first came to India and met the Mother, I was barely nineteen years old. Right from the beginning, I was amazed by the simplicity of the Indian children of the Sri Aurobindo Ashram, in school, at play, in sports, in their capacity to experience joy, their unbounded energy, their mental, vital and physical elasticity. It made me look at myself and realize how western and Christian education had harmed me, making me lose the simplicity, the innocence and energy I must have had once upon a time. I then used to write to the Mother, telling her of my anguish; she would smile, I was told, upon receiving my letter and arrange for me on a plate, flowers to which she had earlier given a meaning (she used to say each flower has a particular vibration and aspiration): "aspiration, simplicity, endurance, Divine grace". Today, having matured and touched upon, in some degree, the source of this joy and simplicity, I still say, whenever I address conferences to an Indian audience, that it is a great privilege to be born an Indian, as you naturally inherit qualities which have been practised for millenniums by your forefathers and which are, so to say, imbedded in your genes: tolerance, gentleness, devotion, the ability to smile in nearly all circumstances. I found that many of these qualities manifested themselves in our fellow participants of the TTC.

As for us, we were still quite confused about whether we really wanted to become teachers! "Blessed are those who are confused," says Guru*ji*; but it is not an easy state of mind. We were disciples of Sri Aurobindo and the Mother, lived in Auroville and there was no question of ever going back on that fact. "Feel at home everywhere," Guru*ji* often told us, probably sensing our torment. He would never pressurize us, never ask us to bow down to him, never ask us when we were coming back next time to the *ashram*. Yet, we were still torn by our inner conflict, of "betraying" Sri Aurobindo and the Mother, not understanding that God is one. Nonetheless, finally Namrita and I did our Teachers' Training Course and became teachers, seven years after we were first introduced to the Art of Living. It was one of the most momentous moments of our lives.

People ask: what is it like to be an Art of Living teacher? How does it feel? What do you have to do ? First of all, it is an awesome responsibility, a great privilege and, above all, an honour. I can only speak for myself: I have had a fairly successful life as a journalist and writer, I have interviewed five Indian Prime Ministers, met many personalities, had books published, addressed packed audiences, but nothing makes me prouder than being an Art of Living teacher. It is fine to do well in worldly life, but how can you beat teaching a beautiful knowledge which not only benefits others immensely, but which helps you to become a better person, to touch unknown realms of joy and sweetness and to discover an untapped source of energy in your Self?

So who makes a good teacher? I would say, one who is faithful, has integrity, compassion and an unwavering attitude to service. Of course, all teachers are not the same: there are those who live the knowledge and others who deliver the knowledge very well but live it only partially. Some have developed many talents, others have become more innocent. Unlike in any other group or organization, here teachers are from all backgrounds, religions and nationalities. It is like a bouquet of assorted flowers, or as we sometimes jokingly say, "a box of assorted nuts" — the serene and quiet Bharat; the loud and bubbly Vikram; the gentle and shy Anurag; the strong and commanding Vinod and the blonde and delicate Nathalie! So diverse are the people and their tendencies, yet they all feel at home with Sri Sri, which is a phenomenon in itself. I marvel at his patience in dealing with them all.

I sometimes wondered how Guruji would select anyone and everyone as a teacher. I used to feel that teachers should have some basic talents, qualifications or standards. I was proved wrong. I came to understand that it is not the talents that really mattered — and this is the most important point — it is the devotion in a teacher that really makes a difference. Many lecturers and professors give scholarly discourses, but they don't make an impact on one's life; but here a teacher delivers the simple truths in life and brings about a definite transformation. Guruji commented once in a teachers' meeting that "do not use knowledge for your mistakes, but as an umbrella". When asked by someone why he keeps creating new teachers, when some of them may not be of the highest calibre, he answered, "You can never judge anyone, because you do not know what diamond is present where.... Truly, the world is diverse: some people may grow by teaching and each one can guide everybody else to whatever extent they can." In conclusion, being an AOL teacher is like carrying an invisible badge on your chest, which makes you as you feel, "I carry an invaluable knowledge, I help in establishing a happier and more harmonious humanity, I am the flag bearer of a new world order. Blessed am I to have been chosen amongst so many."

And it is teachers who form the backbone of the Art of Living movement, through whom Guru*ji* reaches out to so many people. They are his ambassadors, the carriers of His message, and the instruments of His force. Who then are Sri Sri's teachers?

Kishore saw Guru*ji* for the fist time in 1985 in a Basic Course where he arrived because he was impressed by the brochure that said, 'Come and meet your Self'. Thinking that Ravi Shankar, the sitarist, was conducting the course, he found Guru*ji* himself teaching what is now known as the Art of Living Basic Course. The introductory forty-minute meditation was so powerful, that he completely lost track of time. He was working as an engineer then, travelling all over the world but he started organizing Basic Courses. A couple of years later Kishore attended an informal Teachers' Training Course — the first one ever — which was taught by Guru*ji* himself. The notes taken by the participants formed the TTC Manual. Kishore then started teaching the Art of Living Course — only two people to begin with, but slowly the numbers kept growing. He shifted permanently to the *ashram* in 1991, which was an exhilarating but demanding time. He, along with the other people there, used to do a lot of physical work, from digging holes for planting trees, to carrying pipes. When I asked him what he considers to be the biggest miracle Guru*ji* ever performed, he said, "Love is the biggest miracle! How tears turn into smiles in seconds by being with him, how unfriendly people turn out to be compassionate!" Kishore fondly remembers how once while travelling with Guru*ji* by plane, a particularly rude lady turned friendly and warm after just one glance from Guru*ji*.

It was *seva* time — I was watering the plants. As I watched those fragrant jasmine flowers, it occurred to me how they grow on their own — all that we can do is water them a little bit! The same is true in our life. I realized, with knowledge as the nourishing water, life starts bearing flowers like this jasmine plant. I saw Sharmila, who teaches the Art Excel and Young Adult Courses, playing hide and seek with kids. I remembered what Guru*ji* often tells parents: "Your concern is how soon your kids will grow up. My concern is when you will become kids again!" When I first heard it, it sounded ridiculous, but now I know how much sense it makes. The way Sharmila could harness youth energy here was impressive — the teenagers seemed to have overcome inhibitions — they were communicating freely with people of all age-groups. I talked to Sharmila about her journey with Sri Sri.

"There is so much I want to say about my Guru — feelings are so profound, words so inadequate. We have received so much from Him — so much love, grace, knowledge, joy, the nectar of life. Life has been transformed so miraculously, every moment is so breathtakingly beautiful, that the only wish seems to be to share everything. Life is gorgeous, life is fun and I am in eternal gratitude to my Guru who straightened me out; brought me out from my web of fear and insecurities, and opened in me a fountain of love, joy and enthusiasm. He has made me aware of the sheer magnificence of our lives, of the human body, of our very existence. Events continue to happen, but now they do not shake me."

A little later, I came upon a giggling gang of Art of Living teachers and decided to take them all out for a pizza, hoping to get more insights into Sri Sri's life. At the restaurant, one by one they started telling their stories and were so enthusiastic about it that sometimes they would all speak together! I was impressed by the diversity of the "assorted nuts" and their unique experiences with Sri Sri.

Urmila Agarwal, an Indian living in Germany for a long time, was tired of her "spiritual shopping" when some Swiss friends invited her to meet an Indian *yogi* visiting Berne in 1988. This is what she had to say: "My Guru has a name, yet He is formless, eternal beyond time and space. He is much more than this. I know Him and yet I do not know Him. What I do know is that He has given a meaning and direction to my life and brought fulfilment to it. In His presence, I experience the Almighty who dwells in every heart. A touch of Him sweeps away karma of lifetimes, burns away ignorance and brings divinity to shine through human beings.

I used to think that the Guru-disciple connection was also a type of relationship. With Guru*ji* I have experienced that it is beyond all relationships. It is multicoloured and multidimensional, because it is the relationship to one's own reality, the Truth. He is everything for me. He is my parent and my child. He is my brother, my sister and my friend. He has cooked and served me when I was tired and hungry. He has given me whatever, whenever I was in need, before I even asked for it. He has taken my pain away before it would turn into suffering. He has made me immortal before I die. Him — He has always talked to me in the silent moments — now I can hear him.

In August 1988 when my friends invited me to meet an Indian *yogi*, I was searching for a Guru, someone who would take me into the mysteries of the unknown. It was a point in my life when I had almost given up the search because I could not find satisfaction anywhere and once again doubts popped up in my mind. So, after a second thought, I picked up the phone and called my friends and wanted to have a word with the *yogi*. He answered my questions, his voice was very soothing, and in a few minutes my doubts were cleared by a strong feeling of belongingness and joy. Now I wanted to see him in person, so we drove to Berne. When we arrived there I was a little surprised by the young and delicate looking person clad in white, with a radiant face and an unusually simple personality. For the first time I felt that this was the pivotal day of my life. Still thinking myself very smart, I interviewed him and after spending some hours with him, half-heartedly I left for Basel. But there was something I was very happy about — he asked me to come to Bangalore for the International Advance Course in the month of December. This meeting was very special and powerful, a deep experience of joy and celebration. In fact it was the most precious day of my life."

Arun Madhavan was Area Director with Standard Chartered Bank in Mumbai, looking for "breathing space" amidst his work and life, when he came across the Art of Living Course. The immense benefits from the workshop made him sit up and take notice, and he has since grown to be a teacher and singer. Arun recalls, "I met my Gurudev in the mid-eighties, interestingly, in circumstances linked to breath and music. The place of my work, then, was a prestigious bustling business district, at the vortex of traffic and the attendant pollution. I was looking for freedom to breathe! The Healing Breath Workshop that Guruji conducted gave me that freedom and much, much, more. It opened up my hidden passion to sing *bhajans* and experience the ecstasy of *Nadabrahma*. In the years that followed, I began to capture the many facets of the Guru, but even today, like the proverbial iceberg, I have only seen the tip of it. While discussing the agenda for teachers, he always gets them to think of the '*seva*' aspect in life. Nothing can sum it up better than the spontaneous words he uttered, 'In the Art of Living, we care for the world, we care for you.' I have noticed his approach of helping very ordinary people to blossom into radiant individuals. Whenever someone begins to take a tough stand, he will entreat him to see the viewpoint of the other. He does make people, working with him, cope with the extreme dualities of simplicity and complexity. The remarkable feature of his presence can be seen in the zeal with which children, teenagers, youth and seasoned elders flock around him. He has something to offer to everyone. There is always humour flowing through His conversation.

"Once a devotee, rather embarrassed to talk about his occupation, said, 'Guru*ji*, I am in the liquor business, but I intend to stop it.' Guru*ji* replied, 'Oh! you are in the business of intoxicating people. So am I, but I don't intend to stop it!' I have seen his grace flowing in full measure to all those who work with a selfless agenda. Without any doubt, such a soul rarely walks through our planet. We are indeed blessed."

Michael Fischman, our own Basic Course teacher, was also in the group. Michael remembers his surprise when he first came to the *ashram* in 1991. "There were no trees, no buildings, just a few *kutirs*, and a thatch roof hall," he says. "We were preparing for an Advanced Course that was to happen that summer. I was a doubter. I couldn't understand how two hundred people could come to the *ashram* and stay. Gurudev said that it would all just happen. At the time, we just had enough roof space to accommodate around forty people. Yet somehow, when the time came, two hundred people were accommodated easily! It was the most amazing thing, a magical experience. There was enough food for everybody. There were enough beds for everybody and there were no complaints! When I returned years later, it was like coming to an oasis. The transformation was mind-boggling. How did all this manifest from land that was just rock? It can only be the grace of the Guru. Over the years of teaching thousands of people, I have been witness to so many experiences of participants. Some Christians have the experience of Christ during their *Sudarshan Kriya*, while recently, in the Middle East, people experienced the 'Koran reading' happening during the *Kriya*."

John Osborne, the bubbly guitarist entertaining our group, was a successful stock broker in the US when he met young Sri Sri for a few moments. In those moments, he intuitively felt that he had come back to his teacher, and attended the Art of Living Course with his wife that weekend at Santa Barbara. "I remember so clearly the day I met Gurudev," he told us. "Within the first five minutes of being in His presence, I experienced an explosion of pure joy. Even though I had been in service to another spiritual teacher for fifteen years, in just five minutes, I felt closer to Gurudev than I had to my teacher in all those fifteen years. Huge waves of gratitude and relief swept over me! As a child, I had felt the protective presence of Christ. As I grew older, that presence had faded. I thought I had lost it forever, but the moment I saw Gurudev, that vibration immediately made its presence felt. Somehow I knew that I had been graced to meet someone who has attained the highest consciousness that is possible to experience in the human form. My wife and I took the Basic Course in Santa Barbara that weekend, and another in Los Angeles the next weekend, and then another in San Francisco the next! The courses were so lively! A week later, we found ourselves in silence on an Advanced Course in Quebec.

Gurudev is fond of changing roles right in front of our eyes, playing a mischievous trickster one moment, then appearing in the evening as a Divine Mother, cooking dinner for all of us and, still later, becoming stern, strong and dispassionate in the face of a misbehaving devotee. He has a total knowledge of His devotees that can either be comforting or startling. From my first days with him, he told me things about my past that I had never shared with anyone, and he often appeared to know me better than I knew myself. He somehow keeps individual track of all the hundreds of thousands who consider themselves his devotees. Often he will say, "_ is thinking of me now," or "_ is going through a hard time," or "_ is in pain," even though that person is thousands of miles away. His presence goes beyond his physical form.

Hailing from the royal family of Thrissur, our good friend Raghu Raj Raja was an ardent communist as a student. After doing Art of Living Courses, he found the common roots of "caring and sharing" between communism and spirituality. "I first heard about The Art of Living in 1992 from my friend Narayanan, and attended an introductory talk by Dr. Eberhardt, an Art of Living teacher from Germany. Though very impressed at that time, I promptly forgot all about it. A few months later, I heard that there was a TV interview with Sri Sri Ravi Shankar. Something stirred within me, but I had to attend a meeting of a student body closely associated with the Communist Party in Kerala. There were about a score of us in the meeting. As the time for the TV interview drew near, I lost interest in the proceedings and started thinking of a way to sneak out. I was initially hesitant, worried that my absence would be noticed, but I decided that I would go to watch the interview; I did, and I liked what I saw, yet, with my busy schedule, once again I put him out of my mind. The next year in January, I chanced upon a small news item that Sri Sri Ravi Shankar would be in Trichur, at a place very close to my house. I rushed to the venue and found that he would be there at 7 p.m. for a *satsang*. I did not know what a *satsang* was yet I was there at the appointed time. Sri Sri came, sat, spoke a few sentences, but he was quite unlike my idea of a guru for he had none of the expected high-handed behaviour. He was very simple, very natural, as though he was one of us. It was love at first sight! He then sang *Shivoham* and we all sang along with him. I really loved it — the words, and the tune stayed on with me long after Gurudev had left. Many people went up to meet him, but I felt shy and stayed in my seat, even though I was drawn to him. The whole of the next day was spent just waiting for 7 p.m. to arrive. I even excused myself from a family outing so that I could be there at the *satsang*. Gurudev floated in by 7.05 p.m. His talk was inspiring — I was soon to realize that His talks are never anything else. After the *satsang*, once again people queued up to take his blessings but I stood where I was, gazing lovingly at him. As Gurudev passed by, he smiled at me.

"My first event at the *ashram* was the *Rudrabhishek puja*. I initially wondered why he had to perform such a ceremony. This was the 20th century, wasn't it? Still I attended and was totally entranced by the light and beautiful manner in which he conducted it. It was a unique and beautiful experience, quite unlike *pujas* that I had experienced elsewhere. By now, deep within my heart, I knew that all I wanted was only to be with him but I didn't say anything. I went to the ashram for *Navaratri* that year with a big suitcase. At the end of that week, Gurudev said I could stay on at the *ashram*! He said, 'This is your home. Be here, be happy. Celebrate.' This was when the growth really started happening in me. He put me through so many different situations. I failed here and there, but slowly I became stronger and more aware."

A gemmologist by profession, Sangeeta Jani was designing fashion jewellery in Mumbai after studying in the United States. Looking for life beyond the humdrum existence, Jani attended the Art of Living Course. As she progressed through the Advanced Course, being of service appealed to her, and she took to teaching the *Divya Samaj*

Nirman (Creating a Divine Society) Courses to encourage volunteerism and service. "Obviously there is no knowing the guru, she told us in her high society Bombay accent. The only way I know him is through the way I feel and the experiences I have had around him. But each time I thought that I came a little close to knowing him, He would show me a new aspect and confuse me. My first experience with him was an experience in itself. In December 1992, one evening as I stood in front of the mirror, 'painting' my face for another routine evening out, I thought to myself, 'How can I follow a herd of people who make a lifestyle out of working, partying and shopping? This is definitely not why we were created. There has to be another reason.' I looked around and prayed, 'I know you are here. I know that you are aware of all my actions and thoughts and you know me better than I know myself because you created me. I am asking you for guidance. Show me the path and the reason for my being here. Please let me be a vehicle for your will, who or whatever you are. Please talk to me.'

"A few days later, an acquaintance asked me if I wanted to do a course called the Art of Living. Taking this as a divine message, I did attend, and I loved it! Next I wanted to go to Rishikesh for the Advanced Course. As anticipated, my parents refused to let me go to a strange place all alone, so I gave in. But the next morning a strange phenomenon occurred. Totally unexpected, my father himself asked me to go and have a good time. There was a bomb scare at the Delhi airport the day I arrived. Unfazed, my only thought was to meet him. He was sitting in a car. He turned around, looked at me and said, 'So! You are here.' He was expecting me! I felt all the tension leave my body and sensed that I was being drawn into a kind of love that I had been looking for. I knew instantly that my life would never be the same again. I was here to serve.

"Soon my birthday was approaching. 'What's the big deal?', I thought. Another year, another birthday. It would have been nice if I had a boyfriend. I would have had a nice romantic evening. Surprisingly I got permission to arrange a *satsang* at my house, when Guru*ji* would be in town, on my birthday! I finally had something to do. Yet, strangely, I felt a tinge of regret that I would not be able to have a night-out with my friends. The day finally arrived and Gurudev walked in! He did more than any human being could do to make it the most interesting birthday I had ever had. We had a great *satsang*. All my friends who were allergic to the word guru, sat there with tears of love and joy in their eyes. They had experienced deep love. That is when I realized that when you have a guru, the extent of his love is unfathomable. There could be thousands of people around him, but he is constantly aware of each one of us. He ensures all our desires are fulfilled even before we realize them."

The "naughty" boy of our group, Naushad, who hails from an affluent Muslim family in Mumbai, found the Art of Living Course to be a wonderful therapy. "I used to suffer from kidney stone attacks, which were frequent and painful. A few days before I was to have an operation, I took the plunge and did the Advanced Course. After completing the course and practising the *Sudarshan Kriya* for about three weeks, I went for my pre-operative check-up, where it was diagnosed that the stone had disappeared." Amazed by this phenomenon, Naushad did the Teachers' Training Courses, and he now does what he likes doing best — teaching the Art of Living Course in Pakistan.

Vinod Kumar was born and raised in Kuwait where he led a rather boisterous life until he chanced on Guru*ji* at a Bangalore Management Association meeting. Vinod has had some of the most incredible experiences with Guru*ji*. "What I love about my relationship with Gurudev," he told us in his booming voice, "is how he creates an event for everything that he wants to teach us. He told me once that Krishna had said to Arjuna, 'Whatever is charming in the world, I am the charm. I am the attraction itself, behind the event.' Once I attended a fashion show at Delhi and later, went to the venue where Gurudev was staying. At about 8.00 p.m., Gurudev gave *darshan*. Outside his room there was a raised pathway about two feet high, with a lawn on either side. There were about a hundred people waiting on each side when Gurudev came walking out onto the pathway. It was an astonishing sight. Never in my life had I seen anything like it. It was nothing less than God coming down to earth. Such majesty, beauty, radiance and those flowing robes... it was a sight to behold, the way he carried himself that day. Then he looked at me and winked mischievously. No words were spoken but since then on, I have never felt the desire to go to a fashion show.

"One day in 1992, we were driving with Gurudev to Itanagar in Arunachal Pradesh from Tejpur Airport. Along the way, we stopped for a while and Gurudev suggested that we both go for a walk. About five minutes into the walk, Gurudev said, 'Let's go into one of those houses.' I assumed he wanted to rest so I pointed to one of the better houses on the road. Gurudev said 'No, maybe another house,' and we kept walking. After a few minutes, I spotted another inviting house which had several air conditioners mounted in the windows. I said, 'Gurudev, this seems to be a convenient place to rest. Let's go into this one.' He replied, 'Let's keep walking.' After a few more minutes, he pointed toward a shabby ill-kept dwelling and said, 'Why not go into that house?' Despite my protests, he started walking towards the house and I followed him to the gate. On the right-hand side was a big hut. Looking inside, we saw pictures of all the local gurus and deities. As we walked towards the main house, a lady came out and greeted us. We exchanged pleasantries. As we were leaving, Gurudev turned to me and asked 'How much money do you have in your pocket? Give all of it to this lady.' I was surprised at the request but I fished seven hundred and eighty rupees out of my pocket. As I was giving it to her, her son came running from the back of the house crying, 'Mother, I did not get the seven hundred and fifty rupees I went to borrow.'

'Don't worry son, we have the money now!' the mother gratefully replied. It turned out that the boy's father was in the hospital and they desperately needed the money for medical expenses. That day I learned a valuable lesson: this is how God comes in many different ways to a devotee, in time of need."

The only one who had kept silent during this boisterous evening was Prashant Rajore, a chemical engineer from the Indian Institute of Technology, Mumbai. Prashant was healed of his asthma and shyness after the Art of Living Course. "Before coming to the Art of Living I was a very angry person, and at the same time very shy," he agreed. "I had few friends and hardly used to talk to anyone, as I lacked self-confidence. On top of that, I was suffering from asthma. One fine day, Bawa (a fellow student from IIT and a future teacher) just said: 'Come and do this course. You will learn some breathing technique which might help you with your asthma.' For two months I could not do it, because I could not arrange the Course fees, but it was always at the back of my mind. Finally, as I went home one weekend, somebody gave me a sum of money. I don't know who it was, but I just put it in my pocket and as I sat in the train, I would feel the money and I thought, 'That takes care of the Basic Course and I can spend on some travelling and food, etc. I don't have to worry about anything now'!

"The next day, I went for the Course which was outside the IIT campus in Dadar. I was very very stiff and felt very shy. I started looking for Bawa, but he was not there; then I saw Dong (nickname of Harish Ramachandran) — at last a familiar face ! So I went up to him and just stuck with him. During the first *Sudarshan Kriya*, I suddenly smelt some very beautiful fragrance and I thought the teacher might have lit some *agarbatti*. Then I started feeling dizzy and lost awareness, which made me believe that they were using *agarbatti* for putting us in an unconscious state. When I woke up, people were already talking about their experience, but I just kept quiet and did not share anything. Then I had some problems and Bawa, who had become a teacher, took me in his course. After the first *Kriya* Bawa said I was almost dancing. After the second session, suddenly when I looked to one side I saw Guru*ji* walking in and thought, 'Oh... this is the person I have wanted to meet for a long, long time.' I had always had this feeling that some guru was going to come into my life and I would have to go with him. There is a temple opposite my house, where *Shankaracharyas* and other gurus used to come. My father was a trustee so he would take me in just to look at them, but I never felt a resonance with any one. But when I saw Guru*ji* the first time, I knew this was the person. And then he just came and sat in the course. But when he started looking at me persistently, I got more and more stiff and conscious. When it was over, I heaved a sigh of relief. But Bawa took me to the house where he was staying and I found myself with him practically alone. Again he started to look at me and I got more and more embarrassed, but he kept smiling at me.

"There was a *satsang* that evening near that house and I found myself enthusiastically singing *bhajans*. Then he said, 'Anyone has any questions?' So people started asking him questions and I had these two questions that had bothered me for years. But still I felt shy and kept silent. Then he was talking and suddenly I realized, hey! this is the answer to my first question after a while he looked at me and said, '*Samjhe* (understand)?' But I thought this was a coincidence, and though if he answered my second question, then I would believe it. And sure enough, after some time, I realised that he was talking about my second question! Again he said, "Understood?" and looked at me. I thought, this person is very dangerous, and now I can't run away from him! After *satsang*, as he was leaving, I just went and touched his feet."

Rajshree was also with us that night. I have carefully observed, judged, doubted, disagreed and even fought with Sri Sri, she said. "After all, having been a lawyer, that too, a prosecutor for the Los Angeles District Attorney's office and the United States Attorney's office, judging and analysing came easily and naturally. It has never been easy for people to recognize the Divine. During the life of Krishna only three knew of his 'essence', only twelve recognized the Christ, and a few recognized the Buddha. I am sure the biggest quandary of the enlightened is revealing the ultimate truth.

"I have been travelling around the world for twelve years teaching and spreading the knowledge, wisdom and techniques of Sri Sri Ravi Shankar. In my travels, I have met many sceptics who decide at first glance that 'this' is not possible. There is an immediate judgement. People have a need to find an inherent weakness either in the teacher, the 'technique' or in him. It is the nature of the mind to hang on to negativity. My response has always been the same. To smile and to know that doubt is always about positivism. This is one lesson I have learnt from Sri Sri. We doubt in the honesty of people not in their dishonesty. We doubt in our capabilities and not in our weakness or incapabilities. Somehow people associate spirituality, guru and service with being irrational and illogical. True science, and true logic requires a personal experience. A fair exposure to the Art of Living Courses, a few days spent in silence looking at one's self, is enough to truly come to a reasonable conclusion. I have personally taught thousands of people around the world, from all religions and backgrounds and I have yet to meet a person who didn't benefit beyond words. Prophets come and go but the egoistic person waits for the future and glorifies the past. By hanging on to the Christ and the Buddha of the past we create division and conflict. Sri Sri and the Art of Living are about the present, unity and harmony. It is about the simple truth that behind every desire is the search for joy, the search to appreciate life. Eating, sleeping, procreating and collecting things is merely existing; appreciating every moment fully is the art of living."

It was well into the night, and the pizzeria joint was shutting shop. As the rather unique "family get-together" drew to an end, I felt as though I had lived the lives of these many teachers, fired by an inspiration called Sri Sri. A guru with a mission: to make life a celebration.

CHAPTER SEVEN

THE FRAME THAT
HOLDS THE PICTURE

Enlightenment is the journey from the head back to the heart, from words back to silence, getting back to our innocence in spite of our intelligence. Knowledge should lead you to that beautiful point of "I don't know."

*Y*OGIS, SAINTS AND SEERS ARE A GREAT MYSTERY TO the human mind. How should one understand them? How can one analyse them with our limited intellectual capabilities? And then, how does one define the Divine? And put him on paper? Our small mind is quite incapable of comprehending the vastness, intricacy and immense love which is behind each of his human incarnations. Besides, it perpetually doubts, particularly when it is in the presence of the Divine. How many recognized Christ for what he was in his lifetime? How many recognized the Buddha? Doubt has always been the principal impediment to spiritual progress and this holds particularly true when we are in the presence of gurus, as we have a tendency either to question their divinity, or our own perceptions of them. Each Master is an expression of Infinity as is our consciousness. But we like to label ourselves and so also our Masters.

Sri Sri is label-less, he is a guru to one, a friend to another, serious one moment, mischievous the next. You cannot contain him in a book. Being with him, all the labels start to drop off and freedom dawns. In his words, "Only when we are free, can we bring freedom to others." He sets the example in many different ways. Namrita and I, of course, have had our share of doubts regarding Guruji and even now there are times when I cannot fathom some aspect or other of him. Yet, our itinerary is interesting because it is one of "doubting witnesses", who slowly, with their own eyes, have observed one or other facet of him, which makes him so special. Here a few attempts at putting down fleeting impressions of Guruji, both mystical, as well as worldly. Of course, they are mine and I hope I will be forgiven if at times I appear to err, or even be slightly irreverent.

Sri Sri the Mystic

Whoever wants to witness the divinity behind Sri Sri has just to watch him meditate: nobody can cheat at that game! I remember a very old and wise swamy, who, seeing Guruji slipping so easily into meditation, tried to imitate him, but he could not do it, however much he tried. After some time, he invariably started fidgeting, moving his hands, opening his eyes... Guruji can stay immobile for hours and you can actually watch him going more and more inwards — his eyes reaching upwards, his consciousness slowly leaving us, his hands and body becoming very still and reaching planes which are not accessible to us. The mystical air that surrounds Guru*ji* during *puja* and at *satsangs* is unpretentious. The whole environment becomes so homely and comfortable, that you become like a child. Sometimes in *satsangs* his body goes into different types of postures or *mudras*. In those moments the atmosphere becomes charged, though it is not an everyday phenomenon. It certainly happens on *Navaratri* — the festival days of Mother Divine and *Shivratri* when people gather from all over the world. It is an intense electrifying experience. I have watched him in public *satsangs* attended by thousands of people. He has greeted each one with the same smile, with no sign of weariness. Every Monday he himself sits and does the *Rudra Puja*. When asked, why do the *puja* if he himself is divine, his reply was simple, "*Puja* is a play of the divine with himself."

On a particular day in October/November (Dusshera), Hindus worship cars, tools and anything they can lay their hands on, including a simple screwdriver. Their belief is that the divine dwells in every atom, a true understanding of the all-pervasiveness of divinity. It sounds ridiculous from a western point of view, yet its depth has its own beauty. The Vedic chanting by the young boys and the melodious music from the ladies in colourful attires, the beating of drums and musical instruments all add to the magic of the festival. I have always been amazed by the richness of India and its spiritual wealth. Sri Sri goes into silence at this time for a few days. *Yajnas*, (Vedic rituals) for peace and harmony are performed at the *ashram*. On the last day, as the atmosphere has been thus so incredibly charged with energy, devotion and a sense of timelessness, the *kalash* (urn) of water, which seems to have a life of its own, is ceremoniously carried around the *pandal* with Guru*ji* in front. People join their hands in prayer, some even cry; one cannot miss the flow of grace at these times. There seems to be a common belief that people's wishes get fulfilled, though I have not heard this from Sri Sri himself.

Raghu, who has spent time at length with Guru*ji*, vouches for his equanimity. He has never found Guru*ji* affected or ruffled by anything in his long association with him. I have myself noticed how people rush to garland him, put a crown on his head, dive to touch his feet, pull his cheek, or touch him. The constant attempt at grabbing the Master's attention and love by the disciples, this competition for one look of him, one smile, a few words, is taxing. But in spite of all the chaos around him, Sri Sri retains a very profound and deep silence, an unfaltering smile that never gets disturbed. I often wonder how this little man can handle all that day after day! And he is the same with everybody, from the most lowly to the Prime Minister, from the senior teacher to the new seeker. There is a child-like glee on his face, while opening a gift pack or meeting someone new.

It is an unforgettable sight to watch Sri Sri walk through a *darshan* line. It is as if a cloud of love is floating around him. For many it is a dream come true; for some others it is a moment of confusion where all their concepts of gurus are shattered. Sri Sri is not a very demonstrative person. Yet there is no doubting the immense love he is constantly exuding to everyone around and to the world in general. You start noticing it little by little: you feel low or depressed, he passes by and he just looks at you once and immediately after, you become aware that you have lightened up, that there is joy and peace within you. Sometimes, for no reason at all you feel like crying in his presence: these are not tears of sentimentality or sadness, but the inner being which is suddenly awakening in you and seizing your external emotional self. That Sri Sri has been a peoples' person was evident right since his school days. His sister Bhanu invariably recalls instances of students from senior classes in his school coming to him for counselling and guidance in personal and academic areas.

How does one notice the love of Sri Sri — and fall in love with him? By watching him — in meditation, in *samadhi*, with his disciples, noticing his untiring attention for everybody, his boundless patience with his devotees, his selfless dedication to every aspect of life that needs to be addressed. Usually, a relationship with a great loving, realized and selfless guru does not fail us like a human relationship: gurus never demand anything from us and are constantly giving. In fact, there are five aspects which blossom in you at the contact of a genuine guru: joys well up, lack of anything disappears, sorrow vanishes, faith grows and knowledge becomes strong. But for this to happen, your devotion for the guru has to be spontaneous, free, childlike, ego-less. And wow, how devotees love their Sri Sri. And they don't fall in love but, rise instead.

The Human Master

From a human point of view, Guru*ji* possesses unsurpassed qualities. He has, for instance, a phenomenal memory: he never forgets a name, although he says it occasionally happens to him! The man must have millions of devotees today, but he remembers a face seen two years ago and will have always a kind word of welcome for you, querying about your comfort and asking about whatever you are doing. Guru*ji* speaks several languages, yet is never shy to ask for a word that he does not know, or to verify with an American disciple the exact pronunciation of an expression he has just discovered. He says words with relish, as they are meant to convey states of mind, so you have to be very careful when you listen to him, because every word has significance.

His mind is like a computer. Does he think like we do? That is the great mystery of the man. As a yogi he must have a silent and quiet mind, yet he must also have a thinking intellect, because I have seen him clearly plan things, think events out, not one but several at a time, which would leave a normal human being drained and exhausted, provided of course that you can find a person capable of such a superhuman task. He is actually a thinking guru. He chooses his teachers according to his needs. If he needs a teacher in Honolulu, for instance, he will select one, apparently regardless of his or her qualities. Or he will earmark teachers who can be useful in particular fields. The beauty and the secret is that even though it seems to be done at random, even though the person chosen does not appear particularly worthy or fit spiritually, not only does he or she become a good teacher, thanks to the force that Sri Sri puts behind him or her, but probably, he or she was destined to be chosen in spite of all appearances. I count myself amongst those who fit into that category and so will quite a few teachers reading this book. Not only is he an outgoing switchboard, thinking out towards improving the world and bringing love to humanity, but also one to which anybody can connect him or herself. "It is not necessary that the switchboard knows who is connected," he once said. And it is true: whoever thinks of Guru*ji* often feels that he responds in some way — questions get answered, problems get solved. Whoever is distressed or in difficulty often receives help by praying silently. The role of the switchboard is to be the go between you and someone else; this is exactly what Guru*ji* does, like all gurus, by acting as the intermediary between you and the Divine. He is also extremely intuitive. He can fathom the content of a book by reading a few lines, know exactly what state of consciousness you are in, by giving you one glance, or assess a situation by sensing it in a few seconds.

The immense sacrifice that all gurus and saints make when they manifest upon this earth is that while they retain their divinity, they take on something of the earth's pain — they become human and they accept the games and rules of humanity, with its suffering and pain, illness and death. There is actually no need for gurus and saints to be crucified on the cross: they are crucified at every moment by their disciples, who keep throwing their doubts and pettiness on the Master. It is said that Ramana Maharishi died of cancer, because he had voluntarily swallowed all the impurities of his disciples; Sri Aurobindo used to write all night, answering the letters of his uncaring disciples, and went practically blind with it. The worse is that gurus have the power to see the disciples as they are, however they may try to disguise it. The Mother used to tell Satprem, her confidant, that every little vibration of doubt, ill will, or negativity, used to affect her body and that she had to constantly rectify the disharmony which was thus brought upon her. In the same way, one can observe that Guru*ji* never complains, although he must be "swallowing" every day hundreds of little miseries, doubts, petty demands.

Wherever Guru*ji* stays, he plays the host and invariably there is a throng of people to meet him from morning till late at night. There is a deep sense of belongingness in his presence, although everybody acts as if they own Guru*ji*. With people of such diverse attitudes, there is no dearth of bizarre and funny incidents: someone may suddenly decide to stand up and dance, though there is not enough sitting room! Sometimes people elbow others and push their way through to reach the front. People just feel free to be themselves around Sri Sri. On one occasion, Guru*ji* was staying at an industrialist's place in Delhi and there was a volunteer who was controlling access to Guru*ji*'s room. An old lady, a little upset at having to wait, walked straight to the owner of the house, and gave him a tight slap for not letting her meet Guru*ji*! Another time, a man who had lost his own house key while visiting Gurudev, felt free to rest in the owner's bed in the house, and when questioned by the owner, asked who he was!

Vicky Block, an artist from Montreal, met Sri Sri in 1987 and has since been a "puzzled yet staunch" devotee. She has written two books on her years post-AOL, and they are hilarious. Here is what the experience of hosting Sri Sri is like: "What does it feel like to have Sri Sri stay at your house? First you panic. Sri Sri hasn't arrived yet — but the possibility of people tearing around all over your place is more than you can think about, so you just don't. If you are the type of person who never answers the phone, likes to disappear into silence for days, and prefers to see friends away from your 'territory' you might ask yourself what are you doing this for in the first place. The answer to that is that you have no idea. When Sri Sri arrives, so does the rest of the world. Now you have people milling around the kitchen asking for utensils that you have never heard of. There are people ironing, practising the guitar, meditating and waiting to see Guru*ji*. You are so uncomfortable the first day that you go up the street to a friend's apartment to use the shower. You come in wild-eyed, saying all kinds of things like not only 'Why are there people all over the house?' but 'What am I doing with my life?' You don't believe in any of this stuff. You settle down in a soft chair and remark on how calm and quiet it is there. In less than two minutes, you jump up again, and say you have to go home in case you miss something. This is when you realize that the rest of the world has ceased to exist! After Guru*ji* leaves, and when it is all over, I won't say you miss it. But there's a peculiar quality to the silence, a quality that wasn't there before. The house is very light and everything looks so bright, even the things that are still falling out of the cupboards. Having Sri Sri stay in your house doesn't make you better organized or more sociable. But in some imperceptible way, it changes everything. Having Sri Sri stay in your house is heaven and hell — and I'd do it again in a minute!"

In fact, Sri Sri himself is an excellent host. While attending International Advanced Courses, I have seen him take personal care, down to the minute details, of each one of the participants, making them comfortable and at home. He makes sure that even the drivers and watchmen are not neglected and are taken good care of. Once, there was a westerner craving for brown bread though he never told anybody about it. Suddenly, he was delivered a loaf of brown bread by an *ashram* boy from

Guru*ji*'s *kutir*. It's not only householders who come to see Guru*ji*. Often, saffron-clad saints, Christian priests and nuns, Muslim leaders, Buddhist and Jain monks and wise men from other faiths come to seek guidance from him. In the time that I have spent with him, I have seen him totally at ease with a wide spectrum of people. The slum dweller connects with him as easily and effortlessly as the heads of India's largest business houses. He can animatedly discuss an agricultural method with a villager, just as easily as sharing his views on issues of national and international importance with political leaders. A keen learner, he often engages himself in a topical conversation with scientists, as effortlessly as he plays with a child.

The sheer variety and length of one day in the life of Guru*ji* is mind-boggling, as narrated to me by Vinod Kumar: "I once spent a full day with Sri Sri in Rishikesh and his schedule was packed to the minute. He began the day leading the Advanced Course participants and teachers in meditation at 5 a.m. He then interacted with a few of the participants and teachers and then went out to meet with some of the saints who live on the Ganges. He returned to the Vanprastha Ashram to talk to the parents of some Art of Living teachers. Following this, he was scheduled to address a gathering of CEOs, directors and Vice-Presidents to one of the largest corporate houses of India. They had sent a fancy car to drive Sri Sri to the venue of the conference and back. On our return, Sri Sri made the car stop on the banks of the river opposite the *ashram*, saying that he would save

twenty minutes if he simply walked across the bridge
(*Ram Jhula*). To reach it by car was a roundabout drive.
I was with him and we were walking briskly when
suddenly he dashed backwards. He was walking towards
a cow — a cow that was eating some plastic bag! In the
middle of a brisk walk on a packed day, how did he
notice that? With his bare hands, he pulled the plastic bag
out of the cow's mouth, giving it some relief. Meanwhile
I offered to buy some mineral water for him to wash his
hands, but he declined and continued to walk in the
opposite direction holding the plastic bag. I followed,
not knowing what would come next. He had spotted a
garbage bin earlier! After disposing of the plastic bag, he
washed his hands in the Ganges and we proceeded to the
bridge. There he saw a teenager struggling to push a cart
carrying a few sacks of coal up the slope of the bridge.
He realized that the boy was drunk. The next moment,
Sri Sri was pushing the cart along with the boy, till the
middle of the bridge. The bridge sloped downwards and
we thought from there on, it would be easy for the boy.
When he noticed that the boy was still unsteady on his
feet, he asked one of the passers-by to ensure that the boy
reached home safely! As he walked down further, a crowd
collected around him, including some beggars. I began
acting like a bodyguard and attempted to shoo them
away, but Sri Sri stopped me. While he was walking with
them, he answered their queries and reached the *ashram*
just in time for his next meeting — with a group of
prominent social activists and our *Yuvacharyas* (youth

volunteers who are implementing Sri Sri's 5H programme in the villages of India — see Chapter 8.

The Full-of-Fun Master

Of course, Guru*ji* is *fun*, lots of fun. Being with him is entertaining, divine, imaginative, unmitigated fun. Sri Sri loves fun and in fact one of his mottos is "LSD": Laugh, Sing and Dance, a pun for those who prefer the artificial joys of chemical drugs. A greater part of all his courses are devoted to fun: laughing sessions, dancing with music, entertaining techniques... Guru*ji* himself can be like a child: he will wear funny hats offered by his devotees, with no thought about his "image" of a serious guru, will gleefully spray people with rubberized foam, or sprinkle "holy" water on all during *Navaratri*. I find his simplicity and lack of airs extremely appealing and authentic.

In the *ashram* as is the case elsewhere, children are attracted to him like to the legendary Pied Piper. In other spiritual places or places of contemplation and intro-spection, children are often not allowed entry, and if they are, most definitely not near the spiritual head or in the spiritual assemblies. Not so with Sri Sri. I have seen children clamber up to the dais where he is seated, delivering an interesting talk, and in their innocence offering him a flower, garland or a gift. He accepts the gifts without a trace of irritation or impatience and continues as though nothing happened.

In fact once there was this person in the audience who would laugh out loud at regular intervals for no apparent reason, and so much so that Guru*ji* would not be able to continue with his talk. People in the audience wondered why she was allowed in the *satsang* at all, and she was seen as a big obstacle by a majority of the audience. But Sri Sri did not allow the resentment to grow and very skilfully he taught the entire audience to enjoy her laughter and laugh along with her! Not only did the audience become more accepting, the person also learnt to appreciate the sensitivities of those around. Thus, he teaches lessons without actually "teaching" them! This is a phrase I have often heard from people who have interacted with Sri Sri — that they were made aware of their mistakes often without having to suffer the guilt of having committed a mistake!

Another favourite prank of Sri Sri is setting off the alarms at airports while going through the security check — the alarm will go on repeatedly while Sri Sri passes by, but there will be no evidence of metal on his person. He then sports his trademark mischievous smile, while the security personnel have confused looks on their faces. In all major programmes, the organizers plan out things to the minute detail, but Sri Sri evidently creates chaos. Once in Mumbai, there was a crowd of fifty thousand people attending the *satsang* with Sri Sri and elaborate security arrangements were made. Even as the *satsang* was rolling, Sri Sri simply jumped over the fences into the audience. The delighted crowd cheered, while the security and the organizers perspired!

Sometimes, watching Sri Sri defies all your concepts of how a guru should be. He looks like an amalgamation of childishness and wisdom, dignity and mischievousness. A greater part of all his courses are thoroughly entertaining, and you experience a blend of profound wisdom in an atmosphere of fun. "Laugh and make others laugh; don't get entangled, and don't entangle others" is among his most popular quotes. During *satsangs*, he fires water guns on unsuspecting people, showers candies, and sprays celebration foam strings, without at all being image-conscious.

The Baffling Guru

Sri Sri is so special as a master because he works on you without your knowing it. The growth in knowledge is effortless. In another of her very interesting books, titled *Now What*, Vicky writes: "Someone once was arguing with Sri Sri about chanting in Sanskrit when we didn't know what the words meant. How can they have an effect on us if we don't know what they mean? Words are just words and they don't really do anything. Sri Sri then calmly started to insult him, calling him a stupid fool and an idiot. The guy got very upset. 'See,' said Sri Sri, 'look at the effect those words had on you. How can you say words have no real meaning? And those are ordinary words. How do you know the subtle influence of something as ancient and sacred as Sanskrit?' "

Another of Sri Sri's games is to put the wrong people in charge of things. Is this for our growth, or is Guru*ji* a bad manager? Are these just incidental details far below the level of cosmic interest, or is this some kind of test? If someone is good at something, it will be the last thing they are asked to do, or if they are put in charge, it is only to be overruled by someone who doesn't have any experience in that area. New levels of mismanagement are achieved, feelings are hurt, egos and friendships get squelched and still amazing things are accomplished.

On Sri Sri's special style of managing, Vicky comments, "Part of the problem appears to be that Sri Sri specializes in games like putting someone in a position of responsibility without giving them the authority to do anything except fend off complaints, saying, 'Look this is the way it has been decided by the committee, and there is nothing I can do.' While this person is spending all of their time holding back the tidal wave of disruption and advice, some zealot has the nerve to sneak behind them, and ignoring all of the rules and hierarchy, actually DO the job whether they have the qualifications or not." Another American devotee of Sri Sri, Marielle, recalls that once when visiting India, her typewriter suddenly started to refuse to type certain letters. Getting something fixed in India was a problem. First, she asked Sri Sri. He jokingly said Shiva was responsible for it. So after the Shiva Puja the next morning, she took an orange chrysanthemum, put it on the keys of her typewriter, and shut her door so no one would hear her. "Listen Shiva," she said, "I don't know how to pray to you properly, but if you are responsible for breaking my typewriter, please fix it. At least, give me a sign." She reasoned with Shiva for a little while, and then was just about to put in a piece of paper to see if anything had changed, when a disciple called Serjit came in. He had obviously heard her last prayer and glowered at the flower on the keys. "What do you think you're doing?" he said grabbing it. "Don't you know that's exactly what is wrong with this country. For centuries people have been praying to gods for this and that without taking responsibility for anything. If you want something to happen, you have to take action." Marielle decided that this was the necessary sign from Shiva and took her typewriter into town to get it fixed.

Sometimes people come and bother Guru*ji* with very silly questions like, "my cat is sick", "I am going shopping, please bless me so that I do it well", "what should I name my son or daughter" and so on. Once, as I was getting irritated by all these silly questions, Guru*ji* looked at me and said: "Tolerating ignorance is the last *tapasya* (penance)." Indeed, from the very beginning, I observed that my doubts and prejudices seemed to make no difference to him and the way he treated me. There was total acceptance and love from Sri Sri's side, as though giving me the space I required for the doubts to clear. He was only concerned about my comfort and well-being. Initially it was hard to digest, but time proved otherwise.

I was to discover later that he dealt with everyone in the same way — with unconditional love.

The Caring Guru

Talking to people who have been associated with Sri Sri for even a shorter time, one can see him involved hundred per cent in whatever he does. Here are a few testimonies from teachers and disciples.

Philip mentions an instance when a cat came meowing outside his door, as Sri Sri was about to have his food. Immediately he set aside on a plate some rice to be given to the cat. As Philip was about to take it, he stopped him, saying that the rice was too hot and the cat would burn its tongue. He then poured some yoghurt on the rice to cool it down, and set aside some vegetables, after ensuring that they were not too spicy for the feline!

Vinod relates a recent example in Lithuania, where in a public talk Sri Sri had said in response to a question about his message for children, "Leave a better world for them than the way we found it." The next morning, Sri Sri was slightly late reaching the car they had to take for the airport. When asked about the reason for his delay, Sri Sri replied, " I was a little busy cleaning my room." It struck Vinod then that just the day before, this was exactly what Sri Sri had spoken about — leaving things in a better way than you found them.

The depth of Sri Sri's silence, says Bindiya Jain, a close disciple, reflects in the dynamic activity around him. He not only inspires people to do, but he himself works tirelessly without getting stressed. Aware that his assistants cannot cope with his speed, he keeps them in rotation. If you have any doubts about his energy level and capacity, you just need to travel with him for a few days — the doubts will simply vanish. As much as he is blissful, he is alert and active too. He plunges into situations of conflict, and changes the atmosphere to one of harmony. He enjoys cooking, and once in a while, he surprises people by cooking an elaborate meal for them. He loves gardening too.

Once, during the Kumbh mela of Haridwar, remembers Bindiya, Guru*ji*'s black bag with his passport and other travel documents was discovered to be missing. Nitin, who was carrying his bag, had left it on top of a car and forgot to pick it up while leaving. Since Guru*ji* was going to be travelling to Europe in ten days it was important that the bag be located as soon as possible. Despite the best efforts of his disciples, however, the bag was not to be found. Through all this Guru*ji* did not once make Nitin, Sood and Gary (who were also with him) feel guilty for a moment Everybody was getting frantic, but Sri Sri said: "Relax and everything will be okay." At that very moment a phone call came from a person who had found the bag and wanted to return it. (Guru*ji* had earlier remarked that his bag would be found by some angel prior to his departure.) Most of us would have gotten upset and accused the person for being irresponsible. Instead humour and celebration prevailed.

In death as in life, there is also celebration. Neelu's (an AOL teacher) mother Shagun, who was also a teacher, passed away in an accident. Doubt arose in the minds of many of Sri Sri's disciples: "How could this happen to someone who is devoted and on the path?" When questioned, Guru*ji* said, "There is no distinction in the Divine 'as mine', or 'not mine', or to save someone and not to save others. Everybody belongs to the Divine, whether they are on the path or not." Spurred by this, the bereaved family came out of their sorrow and joined the celebration. Everyone sang *Jai Jai Radha Raman*, the last *bhajan* sung during *satsangs*. One hug from Guru*ji* and it was as though their sorrows had diminished. Guru*ji*'s hug has magical qualities in all those moments. As a child remarked it felt like rainbows when he got a hug at *satsang*.

In 1998, during Holi he played with colours and hugged all the eight thousand people who had assembled there. Since then the crowds have become bigger and in some states, as there are upto 3,00,000 people, he has instead started moving amongst the crowds showering rose petals. In the spring of 1987, Guru*ji* was addressing youths in Jhansi. He was to board a train to go to Indore where Mrs Indu Jain, through her contacts had organized a course for two hundred couples of business houses. Upon reaching the railway station, to the dismay of all present, Gur*uji* decided instead to go to Delhi. It had so happened that a young devotee called Choka Reddy, an extraordinarily brilliant student from the Pusa Institute who had recently done the Basic Course, had fallen sick as he had done too many types of meditations. He was admitted to a hospital where electric shocks, sedatives and medication could not calm him down. Nobody could control his madness and everybody prayed for a miracle. As soon as Gur*uji* arrived in Delhi, he went straight to the hospital and held Choka's hand and immediately the boy's violent mood subsided. He started having food and returned to normalcy. Today he is serving in the Agricultural University in Hyderabad.

We have also heard that Gur*uji* once went to Basel, Switzerland, to give a talk to one person! The story goes that he was double booked in France and Switzerland on the same day. Knowing that the talk in France was bigger, he sent Eberhart and Urmila there and chose to be in Basel where the organizer for some reason had cancelled the talk at the last moment. There was only one person in the big hall, other than the four people who accompanied Gur*uji*! They all sat in silence, greeted that one person and came home. That lone spectator, whose name is Marcel, is now an AOL teacher. A musician by profession, he still fondly remembers how Gur*uji* came to get him, instead of attending a lecture for three hundred people!

The Guru who Loves to Celebrate

On one occasion, Guru*ji* made a new song for birthdays. According to him, a birthday is the day when a wave remembers its source, the ocean, and gains the dignity of the ocean. An individual soul with name and form remembers its true nature, as infinity beyond name and form. This is the song:

> *Today is the day the wave remembers*
> *the ocean where it was born*
> *And today is the day we all remember*
> *that this world is our very own.*
> *Happy birthday to you (2)*
> *We belong to you*
> *Happy birthday to —— (name)*
> *We all are your very own*
> *Yes, we all are your very own.*

Birthdays are celebrated with balloons and garlands and Guru*ji* cuts the cake for everybody and throws it saying, "The cake is going to come flying to you!" Winking he says: "If any swami sees me doing this, they may ostracize me." I have never heard him say the words, "I love you", but whenever people say that to him, he echoes it by saying, "Me too!"

During Christmas and Easter celebrations, he is mostly in Europe. There, he enjoys Christmas carols and songs from all different European languages and has been known to hum a couple of Polish tunes and a Taiwanese song as well. Once even the Chinese New Year was celebrated at the Bangalore *ashram* with a traditional deity. Guru*ji* loves diversity and he urges people to maintain diversity of culture and tradition. He is thus deeply concerned about religious conversions in Northeast India, where the inhabitants are fast forgetting their tribal culture. He says that the loss of tribal culture is a loss of world heritage. His slogan is, "Deepen the roots and broaden the vision." This is why he wants the tribals to progress in modern thinking, but at the same time value their ancient traditions. For this purpose, he has opened around a hundred charitable schools in tribal areas. It was during the search for a suitable location in a remote area for one of these schools, that he lost two of his dear disciples, Nandita and Nityanand in an accident. There was an unmistakable pain in his eyes, yet he managed to make the whole atmosphere lighter.

The Management Guru

The Art of Living workshop is now taught in over 130 countries and The Art of Living Foundation is now the largest NGO in the world. It has seen a phenomenal expansion in the last decade considering that Sri Sri did not allow any publicity for his courses and meetings till 1995. It now comprises hundreds of Art of Living teachers, thousands of organizers and millions of followers. I am sure modern day organizations would be eager to know the secret behind its growth. How does the organization work? What is Sri Sri's management style? Sri Sri has been involved in a regimented organization long enough to know its drawbacks. In his own words, "An organization should be like a picture frame. The frame should not eat away the picture." In other words, just as without a frame it is not possible to hold a picture, without an organization, any work, whether spiritual or social, cannot happen. At the same time, if the organization becomes too regimented, it is like the frame eating the picture away. Thus, Sri Sri's organization has a loose structure which allows lot of freedom and creativity and wherever there is a flaw in the working, Sri Sri's attention immediately goes to it. This organisational structure can prove to be a very good model for the corporate sector because work happens, not through motivation, but by inspiration. Sri Sri often encourages people to take up leadership roles and not just remain as followers, so that they become aware of their abilities. Though sometimes this creates chaos, he loves chaos because, as he says, "chaos creates bliss". Through all this you never see him get angry and it is with a smile that he does all his mischief!

In India hundreds of thousands of people come to his *satsangs* and the way they are organized is simply amazing. For example over 300,000 people were in Surat (26 February 2001), over 200,000 in Ahmedabad (28 February 2000) and more than 400,000 in Cochin (17 February 2002). In Kerala over a period of five days, he addressed close to a million people. I was fortunate to travel with him in Kerala and see the amount of devotion in these folks. Though there may be internal squabbling and ego-trips all vying for the attention of Sri Sri, once he is there, it seems as though all the differences have dissolved. Once he addressed the Kerala volunteers, numbering over two thousand five hundred, who had assembled to meet him after working the whole day. When he asked them if they were tired, the answer was a deafening "NO!" And I could see that their faces were really filled with joy, even after having worked so tirelessly.

Is this boundless enthusiasm, this unconditional acceptance of the guru an Indian mindset? Westerners are more organized, more rational — maybe such a thing wouldn't work in the west. All these arguments jostled in my mind till I went to Germany with Sri Sri for New year 2002 and saw for myself how the entire system was working so effortlessly. There also, Sri Sri spends most of his time on individual problems. He has enormous patience to listen to an old lady about her arthritis or parents complaining about their children or... the list is endless. When one gentleman kept pestering him, during the *darshan* line (a time when Sri Sri meets with everybody in the *ashram*), Sri Sri said, "I know, you have already asked the same question eight times today." There was firmness and at the same time compassion, yet there was no anger or frustration in his voice or manner. Another reason for the smooth functioning is that nobody seems to be afraid of making mistakes. I wonder if it is a cultural thing. Is it the same everywhere? Perhaps, but here it is very obvious.

One big problem that arises whenever Sri Sri visits any town is, where will he stay? And who will drive him? Many friends become enemies just on this issue. All the service aspect disappears and selfishness rules when it comes to housing Sri Sri and cooking his food. Another rather unusual aspect of Sri Sri is that he refuses to accept huge sums as donations from the affluent whereas small amounts from a poor person are taken, to make them feel a part of the organization and to give them a sense of self-pride.

Though it is a mass movement, the growth of the individual is not sidelined. Sri Sri often says, "If individuals become strong and brilliant, then the society will become divine." Like everywhere, there are also workaholics in the Art of Living, but Sri Sri keeps them in check: for example our friend Kishore, who likes to do everything perfectly and ahead of time! One thing is for sure, the organization goes crazy sometimes, but still you hardly see any stress. I often wonder what makes people stay awake and work late at night with such cheerfulness. Sri Sri does not set goals or give deadlines for people, yet the enthusiasm that I see in the volunteers, teachers and organizers is unparalleled. At the end of it all, there is tremendous progress both for the individual and organization.

In the AOL movement, the organizers get no monetary benefits other than perhaps some small recognition. All they acquire is the joy of doing something for Sri Sri. As I said before, Guru*ji* seems to be a bad manager for he often creates more chaos and seems to give the job to people who are not very efficient. To him all important serious jobs are also like training workshops. He is more interested in the growth of an individual. Unlike in many organizations there is no hierarchy — at least not a visible one — and confusion often reigns in all departments, from the housing to the publication section. You ask anybody anything and they reply, using Guru*ji*'s knowledge, "Relax and everything will be taken care of," or "Present moment is inevitable". You only get more irritated. This methodology, if tried out in any corporate sector, could be very risky; but somehow it seems to work here, as the individual becomes strong and the organization is growing in leaps and bounds. It is actually interesting to see how orderliness springs out of this chaos.

The Compassionate Guru

This book is not about whitewashing the Art of Living and making everybody look perfect. In the feverishness to be around Sri Sri, it is not uncommon that people forget all his teachings. A few of his teachers often elbow others aside, so as to be able to be walk next to him. Some of his closest disciples will chase him right to his bathroom and will sit glued late into the night, till they have to be shooed out by one of his attendants. In the eagerness to be with him all the time, people forget all decency and above all do not care a hoot about his health, never letting him be alone, never giving him any rest, taxing him all the time, for a look, a *pranam*, a hug, or garlanding him endlessly without a thought for his long hair that gets entangled. Thus, often Gur*uji* has to ask to be locked inside his own *kutir*, so that people think he has gone out. Some of the teachers, in their zeal to do more courses, or get more applicants, fall in the trap of over-selling their guru and indulge in too glib a marketing, putting-up huge posters or hoardings of his photos, which are in bad taste (and of which he disapproves). But somehow, Sri Sri does not seem disturbed by any of it at all. His first principle of, "Accept People as they are", comes through so clearly in the organization. As he said once, "The Art of Living Course is just what life is."

CHAPTER EIGHT

THE STEPS
THAT SPEAK

... pituitary gland has a connection to the hypothalamus gland, which is the seat of consciousness, our mind. Thousands of years ago, people had stated that focus of pituitary gland can affect the whole nervous system in a very positive way. Consciousness works through glands and cleans and brings energy into the immune system, strengthens it and keeps one healthy— "*Swastha*". "*Swastha*" means stabilised in one's self. Health means: mind is centred, focused, free of disturbances and solid.

*W*HAT ATTRACTED ME MOST TO SRI SRI RAVI SHANKAR, as I got to know him better, is the fact that he is a "doing" guru, who practises what he preaches, specially admirable in a country where people are quite passive, and Indian spirituality has often become so divorced from the material, that the physical body of India, its social system, and political system have been left to rot and degenerate. It seems to me that Guru*ji* has come to reform India and to send forth its radiance to the world. For this purpose, of course, he needs to tackle essential features of Indian life which are dragging this wonderful country, the spiritual light of this planet, towards self destruction.

What struck me the first time I went to the Bangalore *ashram*, was that there were only a few servants around and it was the *sadhaks* and inmates who did most of the jobs themselves, including cooking and even cleaning. Some of the guestrooms are personally cleaned and arranged by young ashramites, and tastefully decorated with candles, incenses, photos of Guru*ji*, are worth seeing. The whole *ashram* organization has been taken over, under Guru*ji*'s supervision, by these young ashramites and every time we go there, which is pretty often, there is some improvement: a rocky path has been paved, tiles have been laid somewhere, the place for washing utensils extended, landscaping done (Hi, Hannah and James!). Lots of young boys and girls, who come from affluent families are thus encouraged to do things for themselves, by seeing how in the *ashram*, practically nothing is dependant on servants. And so when they return to society, they bring back a different attitude, which goes further towards changing the system This is the base India needs in order to reconstruct a healthy and just social system.

When the western world talks about India it has a few favourite topics to whip India with, one being the caste system. It is true that it is one of the factors which has led to India's downfall as a great civilization. Yet, once upon a time, whatever India's detractors may say, the caste system was a remarkable setup. As many sages have pointed out, caste was originally an arrangement for the distribution of functions in society, just as much as class in Europe, but the principle on which this distribution was based was peculiar to India. A *Brahmin* was a *Brahmin* not by mere birth, but because he discharged the duty of preserving the spiritual and intellectual elevation of the race, and he had to cultivate the spiritual temperament and acquire the spiritual training which alone would qualify him for the task. And so it was for the *Kshatriya*, who defended his country, the *Vaishya*, who gave it prosperity and the *Shudra*, who discharged the humbler duties of service without which the other castes could not perform their share of labour for the common good. Nevertheless, as Sri Aurobindo pointed out, "the spirit of caste arrogance, exclusiveness and superiority came to dominate it instead of the spirit of duty, and the change weakened the nation and helped to reduce us to our present condition." This is where Sri Sri intervenes again: not only is there no caste, religion or ethnic bar in the Art of Living, which makes it a caste-less movement, a direction India would do well to take, but Guru*ji* has tried to counterbalance this constant harping on the "Oppressed Dalits" by Christian missionaries and Marxist scholars, by having a book published on Dalits, which shows that many of India's revered saints, gurus and Gods (such as Krishna) were from lower castes. In a new Indian society, *Brahmins*, not by birth but by choice, will continue to serve the spiritual and the religious; the *Kshatriyas* will be the professional soldiers, voluntarily, as it happens anyway today; there always will be *Vaishyas* in any society — and business nowadays seems to be the option of many; and the caste of *Shudras* will slowly disappear, as it has been the case in the west, where there are not many servants left — except for the very rich — and be replaced by a better-paid caste-less professional "help".

Travelling in India, I am pained to observe at what is being done to the physical body of this great country: India's ecological condition is catastrophic. Many experts have warned that by the middle of this century there will be no more forest cover left here. Already, hardly eleven per cent of India's classified forests have adequate density, whereas in 1950, one third of India's area was still forested. Each year India loses through deforesting a territory bigger than France, that is nearly two million hectares; of this, only three per cent is protected — and even that three per cent is in deep distress, because of population pressure, big dams (like the Narmada), and industries. India's population will cross the billion-and-a-half mark by 2050, unless a drastic effort is undertaken and will overflow everywhere, stifling any progress, annihilating all efforts. India's cities will be so polluted by their millions of cars that it will be impossible to breathe any more; its rivers will be so poisoned by industries, that all living life will long have disappeared from it. There will be no drinking water left, except imported mineral water. And India will be littered with so much plastic — bags, bottles, buckets — that it will be materially impossible to ever get rid of them.

Sri Sri shows great concern for ecology, for India's physical body: no plastic bags in his *ashram*; food and waste are used to make compost and everything else is sorted out and recycled in different pits. Solar energy is slowly being introduced, trees have been planted by the thousands, Reverse Osmosis water generation is used, food is fresh and vegetarian. Recently, when the Karnataka Government was planning to enlarge the Kanakapura road where the *ashram* is situated, hundred of trees — tamarinds, peepuls, neems — bordering the road, were to be cut, some of them more than a hundred years old. Guru*ji*'s disciples swung into action, writing petitions, meeting officials, posting protests everywhere. Will it save the trees? That's another question. We in Auroville fought against the enlargement of the Chennai–Mahabalipuram–Pondicherry road, now called the East Coast Road, but we could not save hundreds of ancient trees, in spite of going to court. The only thing we were allowed to do was to replant on the side of the new road. Ten years later these trees are already giving shade, a tribute to nature's never-ending good will. Unfortunately, we heard recently that the government is planning to enlarge the road once more ... but a good guru is one who never gives up!

One of the greatest advantages for Guru*ji* is that he knows many Indian languages and communicates well with people from both the north and the south. In the west, the Church plays a major part both socially and politically. But in India, people have a notion that spiritual masters should not play any role in national politics. Sri Sri has mature ideas about politics and some of his advice to political leaders has been greatly valued. He is in touch with the newspapers and asks people around him to read to him good articles while he is travelling or when his schedule permits the same. He keeps in touch with the current affairs in the world and airs his concern on issues like violence, corruption, politics and religion and one of the things that has really concerned him is religious conversions. He has spoken in very many forums on current issues and topics, and his rendering has been brilliant. Concerned with the decline in positive and constructive journalism in India, he inspired senior journalists to come together and start the Sri Sri Centre for Media Studies.

Yet, it is also true that he keeps a distance from politics. This is very unfortunate, as Sri Sri, with such a huge following could work wonders in the political system of India. I sometimes wonder why he refrains from influencing the political system, that is so corrupt and criminalized, with every political party playing vote-bank politics. Why does he not also deal with the media, which is so biased against the Hindus and constantly tries to malign Indian gurus by calling them "Godmen"? Definitely, the fact that a country with such a huge wealth has been under foreign domination for so long, explains a lot. It is also very sad that an aggressive religious conversion by the evangelists is going on at the moment, right under the nose of the Hindu saints, who seem to be oblivious to it. The activist in me becomes so restless.

But every time I bring up the subject to Sri Sri, he simply smiles or changes the topic. There are certain questions to which you can never get answers from him. It can be frustrating at times and at other times it allows you to see something beyond — maybe it relates to some ethereal reason. There are many maniacs who interpret every little move of his and attribute them to some cosmic reason. I am not one of them. And when such questions dog your mind as it often does in my case, I stop listening to any further. As he once said to someone who was pestering him with the same question again and again, "Asking a question is your right and answering it or not is mine." I feel compassion for him. How many questions he is asked and with what patience he listens to them! But my restless mind does not stop asking either. As if he knew this, he once came right up to me in the *darshan* line and asked me to listen to the *Ashtavakra* tapes, a discourse he gave on the treatise by the Sage Ashtavakra which beautifully explains the knowledge of the Self.

I went back to my room and decided to act upon his advice. Immediately, a certain quietness dawned in me. The cacophony of the frogs outside my room appeared musical and I started smiling to myself. It took me quite a few days to listen to the forty-one tapes on *Ashtavakra*, though, for it had to be heard in a group and discussed thereupon. Everybody in the small group would go into intense discussions, which sometimes completely went off track. But this gave so many opportunities to all of us to find out where each of us was stuck. I had heard Guruji saying that the mind was the most entertaining object we possess. If only we could watch it!

One of the criticisms about Sri Sri in the media is that he is a guru of "the elite" and caters only to the rich. It is pointed out that he often travels in a Mercedes Benz, or stays in the houses of his rich disciples. But little do they know that Guruji has actually no car of his own and, that once upon a time he used to travel in rickshaws, or as Kishore remembers "on the back of a scooter" and that he does not mind staying in any humble abode. And what about the crores of villagers, the illiterates, the poor and the sick who come for his blessings or receive the benefits of his many rural projects? Discussed below are a few of his rural projects and schemes for the deprived, the oppressed and the outcasts of society.

Youth Training Programme

One night while at Rishikesh, Sri Sri asked if it was anyone's birthday. Five people stood up. Amongst them I spotted a familiar face — it was Sanjay, a shy and reserved boy, whom I had earlier seen in the Bangalore *ashram*. Everyone was singing the Art of Living birthday song and Guruji garlanded all of them. The next day I saw Sanjay addressing a group of people — it was not the Sanjay I remembered. There was a striking difference in his demeanour. Gone was the timidity — it had been replaced by a confidence that shone on his face. I managed to speak to him around lunchtime and I learnt that he had become a *Yuvacharya* (Youth Leader) after undergoing Sri Sri's Youth Training Programme, perhaps the most ambitious scheme to educate the rural community. Like Sanjay, most *Yuvacharyas* are volunteers, inspired by Ravi Shankar to do service where it is most needed: in rural and tribal areas. Another charitable trust, Sri Sri Vidya Mandir, has also been founded to spread education.

Here are some of the comments of various people having come in contact with this programme. "I was a totally pessimistic person who saw only negativity in everything around me. Depressed in life, I was suffering both physically and mentally. Unenthusiastically I dragged myself around as the days and years passed. The YTP is the best thing that happened in my life. I think this is the most unique programme in the world. It has revolutionized my outlook of life from failure, sorrow and stress to enthusiasm and dynamism. I feel incredibly strong," says Sajda Rehman, a student from Jamshedpur. Ahinsa, another student from Surat, wrote: "Before YTP I was like a kite, whose thread has been snapped, wandering aimlessly in the sky, wanting to rise and soar on the horizon. I was like a machine, who lived because I was alive. I lacked confidence and liked to stay aloof. YTP has transformed my life completely. Now my life has a sense of commitment, responsibility, love and patriotism. I feel strong and am ready to serve the people."

Mr Hanumantesh, a yoga teacher from Shimoga, feels that "After my YTP Course, I realized that I had restricted my life to only one area. Now I can reach farther to every corner of my country — India. YTP has strengthened my drive for service. I can now face any challenge whatsoever."

Remember the devastating earthquake which hit the entire Indian subcontinent on 26 January 2001? The quake, measuring 7.9 on the Richter Scale with epicentre around 20 km northeast of Bhuj in Gujarat, caused immense loss of life and property. The Art of Living Foundation contributed its grassroots approach to helping quake victims, organizing teams of volunteers from around the world, both on the ground and on the Internet. These NGO teams possess the experience, networks, and established centres of distribution in India that proved invaluable in the chaotic relief efforts.

Sanjay told me that this programme had helped him overcome his shyness, and get a direction and purpose in life.

The 5H Programme

Sanjay also talked animatedly to me about the 5-H programme, which, without doubt, is the star project of the Art of Living as an NGO and the vehicle through which the International Association for Human Values delivers a wide array of humanitarian service projects in

India as well as countries around the world. He explained to me that Sri Sri Ravi Shankar feels that human suffering has many faces. In some parts of the world, people live in squalor and abject poverty, without proper sanitation or housing. Unhygienic conditions and lack of proper education about health and hygiene give rise to disease and poor health. In other parts of the world, people may have achieved a decent standard of living, but we find dissension, disharmony, stress, violence, crime and other social ills. In some parts of the world, war has decimated the social fabric and brought great suffering. There is a pressing need for healing at all levels. In each of these situations, the International Association for Human Values, through its 5H Programme, assists in eradicating misery and in transforming society.

For Guru*ji*, "Human life is a great and rare gift, and all people on this planet should have the chance to express through their lives the full potential of their human-ness." This means claiming their birthright to a disease-free body and a stress-free mind, which in turn means living lives that express human values such as compassion, non-violence, generosity, and an ethic of service and caring for all life. Thus, he feels that social transformation begins with a happy and healthy individual who has attained a decent standard of living and has received essential education in health, hygiene, and life skills. Addressing substandard housing and sanitation alone cannot result in the long-term eradication of misery nor bring about a fundamental social transformation.

Education is essential, particularly education in human values. Once the material conditions of living have reached an adequate level, there is a possibility for true human-ness to be expressed in life. A sense of belonging, sharing, non-violence, caring for life, and caring for the planet are among the values that need to be nurtured. The development of human values is essential in creating loving and happy families, cohesive communities, and harmonious relations among all people and nations — a prerequisite for peace, harmony and well-being on the planet. The five elements of the action plan are:

Health: The first step towards a happy, fulfilling life. Yet vast segments of the world's population do not have access to proper nutrition nor medical and dental care, nor have they received even the most rudimentary education in achieving and maintaining good health. The 5H programme has already initiated projects in various areas of India, organizing health care camps which provide medical and dental care to the rural population. As well, medical assistance has been provided to children suffering from polio in a number of regions in Gujarat, India. The 5H medium-term programme objectives are to expand the areas of service, including expansion to other developing countries in Asia and Africa; setting up medical centres in various rural villages; providing ambulances for remote areas; and initiating alcohol/tobacco/drug de-addiction and rehabilitation programmes. Additionally, volunteers provide basic health care education.

Hygiene: Achieving and maintaining good health is difficult where there are inadequate sanitation practices, a lack of clean drinking water, and insufficient means for garbage disposal. Many of the world's poor live in such deplorable conditions.

The 5H Programme is currently addressing this situation in rural villages in India through the simple yet effective means of building toilets, providing borewells for clean drinking water, constructing water storage tanks, and providing garbage bins where needed. Volunteers create awareness about hygiene among the rural population. This programme is being expanded into other regions of India as well as to other developing countries in Asia and Africa.

Housing: Many of the world's poor are homeless, living on the streets or in substandard housing. This serious problem is being addressed by the International Association for Human Values through its "Homes For Change" initiative, under the 5H Programme, which builds modest but durable homes for poor families, at no cost to the recipients. Each home is comprised of three rooms, a kitchen, a bedroom, and a family room, with a separate toilet provided. All homes are built of durable brick and cement. Through "Homes for Change," houses are presently being built for poor families in rural south India. This programme is being expanded to other countries. It costs approximately US $2,000 to build one of these homes in India. Donors can contribute the cost of an entire house for a designated family, or they can contribute the cost of particular items, such as a toilet, materials, or labour. All 5H projects are planned in consultation with the local population to ensure that the greatest needs are met for both individuals and the whole community.

Human Values: There is a growing awareness that the long-term eradication of poverty and human misery requires a fundamental shift in consciousness. Many projects aimed at improving the material conditions of life for the poor have had disappointing long-term results, and have been ineffective in eradicating the roots of poverty. The 5H Programme provides a holistic ongoing framework of education and support that has the potential to lift people permanently out of the trap of poverty and misery. Human values are the hallmark of human evolution and the basis of a peaceful and prosperous world. These values can flourish once basic material needs of a community have been met. Violence, hatred, crime and other pervasive social ills are the direct result of a lack of attention to human values. The foundation for developing human values is a sense of belonging and oneness, which arises spontaneously through the participation of the whole community in the upliftment of each of its members in the context of 5H projects. Also, life-skills educational programmes that emphasize values, as well as multi-ethnic festivals organized by volunteers, all contribute to the development of a sense of belonging and an ethic of service, bringing cohesion to families and communities.

Harmony in Diversity is the overall objective of the 5H Programme. A number of projects are presently underway in war-torn regions of Eastern Europe that focus specifically on this objective. In the aftermath of armed conflict, there is a need to work with survivors to promote healing and restore harmony. The International Association for Human Values has developed a volunteer programme, in collaboration with its partners, to respond to this pressing need in Croatia, Bosnia and Kosovo. The programme provides an opportunity for volunteers to commit one year in helping victims of war rebuild their lives and begin emotional healing. Volunteers receive intensive training in teaching a carefully-designed programme that promotes harmony and healing. As well, the volunteers coordinate service projects to rebuild homes and provide clothing, in liaison with the International Association for Human Values. Sri Sri Ravi Shankar feels that ending violence in society is one of the greatest challenges in today's world. All forms of violence — including youth violence, domestic violence, human rights violations, criminal behaviour, and war — spring from the same seed of hatred. How can hatred be eliminated? The present crisis, says Guru*ji*, "is basically one of identification: How do people see their basic identity? What is their fundamental concept of who they are? Limited and fragmented identification leads to hatred, violence and war." The International Association for Human Values, in collaboration with its partners, provides educational programmes for all sectors of society aimed at bringing about this fundamental understanding, which is the basis of Harmony in Diversity and ultimately world peace.

These values have already been brought to over eight thousand villages all over India through *Nava Chetana Shivir*, an awareness-enhancing programme, at the end of which the villagers take up service projects in their areas. Sri Sri takes intense interest in these programmes and commits personal time in visiting villages, monitoring the progress and providing wise counsel. The ultimate goal is an India that is *Swachha* (Clean), *Swastha* (Healthy), *Sushikshita* (Educated), *Subhadra* (Auspicious) and *Sundara* (Beautiful).

Art of Living for Peace

I found that Sanjay was addressing some other people the next evening, but I sensed a reluctance in him to talk to me about them. After some persistence, he agreed to speak, on the condition that I keep it confidential. The people he was addressing were members of the Ultra-left rival warring groups from Bihar: they were dreaded criminals — one lady in the group had committed sixty murders; two of the men over 250. I thought this was impossible, as these groups had been in the news for committing some of the biggest massacres in Bihar, the land where Buddha was born and were sworn enemies. I was wondering what they are doing in a meditation centre, but found out that Sri Sri had taken an initiative to restore peace and bring about transformation in this troubled land that is Bihar. I remembered also reading about the *Sudarshan Kriya s* effectiveness in conflict resolution and the UN initiative to use it in the Bosnian war.

Naturally, I felt, it must have taken a lot of persuasion and time to get them here, and asked Sanjay about it. He smiled and remarked that it took him six days — two days to reach Bihar, two to collect them, and two to return! Sanjay had visited Rishikesh ten days earlier with a plan to spend his birthday with Sri Sri. While at Rishikesh, he came across the news item about large-scale massacres in Bihar. Inspired by Sri Sri, he went to the heartland of the crime himself, and separately invited the warring factions to visit Rishikesh and meet Sri Sri. At first, the heads of the groups challenged Sanjay to reach the mainland without getting killed in the process — "if he reached unharmed, they told him, they would admit that Sanjay's guru was worthy of their faith"! Sanjay cheerfully agreed, and called them from Patna after reaching there safe and sound. They were so surprised at Sanjay's safe passage through the killing fields, that they kept their word and agreed to come. Naturally, each of the groups did not know about their rivals' coming. And when they first encountered each other face to face after arriving in Rishikesh, sparks flew. "But, says Sanjay, Sri Sri's presence dissolved the conflict and they agreed to take the Art of Living Course together." Over the next few days, the *Sudarshan Kriya*, meditation and the atmosphere of celebration brought about a massive transformation in their attitude. At the end of their course, they voluntarily swore in Sri Sri's presence to give up violence and commit their time to service. Soon after they returned to their territories, they sent contingents of nearly two hundred people to go through the same programme, which had a profound influence on them. It is with those groups that Sanjay was discussing strategies of how to go about the work in the villages.

Prisoners of Fortune

Sensing my keen interest in Bihar, and with the characteristic Indian quality of gentleness to the guest, Sanjay sent word for Indu Sinha, another teacher from Bihar. Indu, a typical middle-aged Indian housewife, told me her story: She was born and raised in Bihar, and had always been saddened by the high criminal activity that goes on there and the number of prisoners that crowd Bihar's notoriously dangerous jails. Keen on making a difference, she took Sri Sri's blessings to talk to the superintendent of Bihar's largest jail and offer Prison Smart Courses for the warring factions who were serving their sentence there. The superintendent, though initially sceptical, agreed to try it out, and what happened over the next few weeks was truly miraculous. The dreaded criminals, who have had histories of multiple murders would air their hostilities aggressively to Indu on the first day of the six-day course. But by the third day, cleansed of their trauma by the *Sudarshan Kriya*, they would melt and cry. Many of them opened up and shared that although they had sworn to kill the people who put them in jail, they were now ready to let go of their past. The police force was so relieved that such an unexpected change of attitude had happened in a place, which was infamous for its many jailbreaks and gang wars, that they opened up many other jails to the programme. This culminated in Sri Sri's visit to the Patna jail in May 2002.

The success story with Bihar criminals inspired the Bombay police to aggressively utilize the Prison Smart Course in their jails. After taking two such courses, Mohammed Afroze, an alleged "Al Qaida" operative who was to blow up the London House of Commons, underwent a complete change of heart. Fellow prisoners found an aloof Afroze transformed into a definitely more friendly, cheerful and relaxed person. He himself commented that "he was promised to go to heaven after death, but he found the heaven right here". Later, he refused an offer to be released from prison on bail, as he had enrolled for the Advanced Course in the jail soon thereafter. This made headline news in most major Bombay newspapers!

I have heard Sri Sri say, "Terrorists are basically good people, as they are willing to put their life behind their cause. They just need the right direction in life." In fact, if you look carefully at Bin Laden's face on the photos, you can see an almost mystical expression in the man. Subsequently, Sanjay told me, several thousand prisoners in Tihar jail too, took the Prison Smart Course, culminating in a visit by Sri Sri there. During the visit, Sri Sri found that a large number of people over sixty years of age and physically weak were held in captivity for alleged crimes. In spite of his extremely busy schedule then, Sri Sri organized that a survey of those people be done, and appealed for general mercy to the Lieutenant Governor of Delhi for their release!

It was well past lunchtime, and the warm sun had already begun its descent. Indu Sinha and Sanjay took their leave, as the young Raghavendra was briskly walking towards the amphitheatre to do a sound check for the evening *satsang*. It was a very still and serene moment. And I wondered to myself how, whatever be the field of activity — be it medicine, journalism, or chemical-free farming — Sri Sri was right there encouraging everybody and giving them his full support. In my long journalistic career, I have seen ample social activists who rake up different issues and create frustration in order to achieve their results. I had often wondered: is there an alternate method of reform, without frustration, anger and dejection? I think I have found it here — the approach of love. The old saying, "Love is the greatest force of transformation" is effortlessly demonstrated here.

CHAPTER NINE

THE
DISCIPLES

In presence of your Sadguru
Knowledge flourishes, sorrow
diminishes; without any reason,
joy wells up; lack diminishes;
abundance dawns; and all talents manifest.
To the degree you feel connected
to your guru, these qualities
manifest in your life.

SRI SRI IS A GREAT GURU, AND HE HAS GREAT DISCIPLES. What is even more remarkable is that many of his disciples are young and talented. Not for Guru*ji* an *ashram* with old feeble *sadhaks*, but on the contrary, many young, bright, luminous souls, whom he often picks up in his Art Excel Courses, bringing them to maturity through subtle personal coaching. Eventually, many of these youngsters become teachers. Western disciples of Indian gurus have sometimes perfected the art of looking warm and good, while retaining inside them a certain hardness. Or in the opposite direction, people, both western and eastern, who have taken to the spiritual path, tend to appear, after a certain age, dour and unsmiling, which comes out of routine, however spiritualized it is, and of the ego of being on the "right" path. Not so with most of Sri Sri's western disciples, although they do not always possess the easiness and transparency which Indians naturally have, because of their spiritualized background: theirs is a genuine warmth, openness, generosity and selflessness.

From Ph.D.s to illiterates, from farmers to MTV VJs, from the slums of Dharavi to the Silicon Valley, Sri Sri's disciples are as diverse as the human race itself. A fair number of them are well qualified with degrees from Indian Institutes of Technology (IIT) and Indian Institutes of Management (IIM), and are typically from a middle-class background. There is a sizeable number of young people from all continents except Antarctica. Many of them did the Art of Living Courses while they were at college, and it touched them in a way all the other education in their life did not: It restored their confidence and enthusiasm, healed them of disorders and gave a sense of direction in their lives. I know for a fact that Sri Sri spends a lot of personal time coaching, mentoring and grooming his young devotees, and so do many of his senior teachers. They have seen their talents blossom forth in Sri Sri's presence — be it in poetry, music, and organizing, programming or designing skills.

Curious to get a closer look at some of Sri Sri's young disciples, I approached Ajay Vig from Delhi, who was in an animated discussion with Vinod in the administration block of the *ashram*, while expecting a guest speaker to address the Youth Training Programme participants. Ajay is the coordinator for Sri Sri's Youth Training Programme under which, as we have seen earlier, rural youth gain vital leadership training to take up responsibility for their progress. Ajay graduated from the IIM, Ahmedabad, which is as famous as the Harvard Business School in this part of the world. "I heard Sri Sri talk about how India's development depended on the improvement of rural youth, as seventy per cent of India is in her villages," he recalls. "Sri Sri's presence inspired me to take up the cause of rural youth instead of just worrying about my bread and butter. I found my talents put to good use in these projects, and grew to become the coordinator of the Youth Leadership Training Programme (YLTP) which transforms unemployed or angry village youth into productive and confident people. The bright sparks from the YLTP are then offered a four-month Sri Sri Rural Development Programme (SSRDP) headed by Vinod. This programme offers vocational training in the areas of carpentry, lathe, welding, organic farming, commercial transactions and office management. Ajay explained "that there is not so much dearth of employment in India as there is a dearth of employability. The skills of physical fitness, the right attitude, and responsibility, initiative and action orientation coupled with office management and commercial skills make the SSRDP graduates highly employable." Ajay futher remarked that "Sri Sri attends to the SSRDP team by paying attention to their growth and surprising them with new uniforms, gifts, sweets. Currently, the second batch of about sixty rural youth is taking this intensive programme."

Sri Sri has also been a source of diverse experiences to his disciples. Hassan Helilian, for instance, was born in Iran, migrated to Canada and as a taxi driver had a bizarre experience with a customer who wished to travel long-distance with him in his taxi. "After working all day, I picked up a customer in the early hours of the morning. He wanted to travel a long distance and wanted to make a deal with me for fifty dollars. I told him that it was not possible and that I would have to put the meter on. He agreed, but once we were on the highway, he started cursing me. Feeling the anger rise in me, I stopped the car. He was quiet for a moment and then, pulling out a gun, he said, 'I can shoot you, kill you, don't mess with me!' For a moment I was petrified; I felt the beads of sweat on my forehead and the tightness in my chest. Then this strong feeling came over me that none could harm me, because wherever I go, I feel the presence of Guru*ji*. I uttered a silent prayer. The man continued to scream at me, when suddenly his eyes fell on Guru*ji*'s picture on the dashboard. He started mumbling, then became quiet. After some moments he asked, 'Who is this man?' I turned, looked straight into his eyes, and replied, 'That is a picture of my guru.' Suddenly he became mellow, folded his hands in 'Namaste', and bowed, first to the picture, then to me. He did this many times and kept saying 'I'm sorry!' Arriving at our destination, he not only paid me my full fare, but I also got a lavish tip!"

Another disciple, Dr. Katherine Kamanda who is a Ph.D. and Professor of World Religions in the US recalled that her mother had witnessed a vision of Sri Sri a day before she was born. "My mother had a difficult pregnancy. She had been quite ill during most of it and had been in a car accident towards the end. In the last month of her pregnancy, she was confined to bed as the doctor was worried that I might not make it. Needless to say, my mother was overcome with fear, and could barely sleep because of her worries. Then, one night, a strange thing happened. She told me that the room filled with a golden light and a Being appeared before her. I have always heard her describe him as wearing a white, flowing robe, having long black hair and a beard. But the most beautiful thing about this Being, my mother would tell me, were his eyes. She said she had never seen such beautiful eyes in her entire life; he didn't say anything to her, but communicated the most exquisite love through those eyes. He just washed wave after wave of love over her with those eyes, removing her fear forever. She always said that she thought he might have been Jesus, but whoever he was, she would never forget him! She never again felt fear in her life ... even to this day. When I was nineteen and in college, I met Guru*ji*. My mother thought I had joined a cult and was worried about me. When I did my *sadhana*, she would hear strange noises coming from my room and wondered who the saint with the long hair and beard in the picture placed with reverence on my shrine was, though she would never actually look at it. Then came a time when she suffered from cancer. She wanted to know who my guru was, what he taught me and what he looked like. When I showed his photo to her, she gazed into his eyes and began to cry. I asked her what was wrong and she answered, 'This is the man who came to me the night before you were born!' "

Michael Adams, an American priest, "felt the presence of Christ in Sri Sri during his first encounter". Subsequently he wrote to Sri, Sri, "Dearest Gurudev, as a priest, I see you at the altar. I have chosen to see you as the living Christ, and I imagine that those who saw Jesus must have experienced him just as we experience you now. I always see you at the altar and ask Your blessings and presence in my masses. God, guru and self are indeed all the same, yet guru is still so special for guru is God in a body. We are blessed and thankful to have your love. I ask for your continued blessings in my life, in all my roles, that I may be blessed and grow to become nobody and then to become everybody. I wish to live in bliss and share it with others, bless and love others with the strength and unity of God, guru and self in realization. You are as close as my heart. But I want more! I want nothing less than to be you!"

Manju Kishinchand from Indonesia overcame her bulimia through the grace of Sri Sri and qualified to be an MTV VJ. "I still remember those days when I was preparing myself to be an MTV VJ. Physically, it was taking its toll. I abused my body and the desire to fit into the MTV image of a perfect slim personality made me go on various diets and spend hours in the gym. As a result I often fell sick, was admitted to the hospital, and frequently the doctors had to give large doses of antibiotics as my immune system had completely given up. Then I met Guru*ji* and spent some time at the *ashram*. It is funny but very few people know what actually goes on in the minds of people who are going through bulimia — the person's mind would be thinking about food and body all through out the day and dreaming about it too. It is a disease that completely wrecks one's mind and of course, one's body. Guru*ji* advised me patiently about my eating habits. He inquired about the functioning of my stomach, and would actually tell me what to do next and how. How the *Kriya* and all the other cleansing processes kept me going, only I know, because on the outside I looked very healthy and beautiful. Before meeting Gurudev, life was an effort, now it is effortless. If a fish is asked to narrate the vastness of an ocean or to describe its greatness, what can it say?"

Iravati Kulkarni, a Sanskrit graduate and singer from Pune considers Sri Sri to be her friend, philosopher and guide. "So often people ask me how I compose *bhajans*! I have no experience of composing music, nor do I hold any special knowledge about it. Whatever *bhajans* have come through me are His creations. And I feel very blessed to be the channel for his songs. '*Parameshwari Jaya Durga*', the very first *bhajan*, came in a prayerful longing during *Navaratri*. I wanted to go to the Bangalore *ashram* since I had heard so much about the *pujas* which happen there during the *Navaratri* celebrations. I could not go. Though physically I was in Mumbai, my mind was in the *ashram*. And during one such night, in my sleep, I heard this *bhajan*. I couldn't wait till the morning. In the middle of the night, I got up and sang it aloud. The words were not mine nor the tune. And yet it was simply the divine grace pouring over me and the first *bhajan* was born. During the *Shivratri* celebrations this year, I silently prayed to Guru*ji*, telling him to send me another *bhajan* so that I could sing it to him. Within the next few minutes, a new *Shiva bhajan* was born! And as I started to sing it in *satsang*, he also started to sing along with me. Everyone looked on in amazement, wondering how he knew the lyrics, when the bhajan was being sung for the first time! For me, he is the embodiment of mother, father, friend, guru ... and much more. He has given me tremendous courage, made me lose my inhibitions, fears and a whole lot of unnecessary burdens that I was carrying around. And his infinite love, compassion and patience has made this entire process so smooth and simple!"

Kashi, a Masters in chemical engineering in qualification, has become a full-time ashramite and looks after publications and the computer systems. "I never knew why, but I had a general feeling that meditation techniques were not for me. Was I not young, intelligent and enthusiastic? And in the midst of all this — meditation? No, this was not for me at all. Yet the day when I went to Khurshed's (my Basic Course teacher) room in his hostel, I saw a photograph of Sri Sri, and instantly felt a deep bond that was beyond explanation, beyond reason and decided to attend the Basic Course in Khurshed's house. The first day of the Basic Course I felt so much at home; it was like returning, recognizing my family. Of course, it was the *Sudarshan Kriya* that really blew me off my feet. By the end of the process I felt a sharp shooting pain in my feet as if someone was hitting nails in my soles. I had excruciating pain, and my body arched all the way as if I would be lifted off the floor. Even though I opened my mouth, no sound came out. Unable to bear it any longer, I opened my eyes a little bit, and what did I see — a figure in white, the same enchanting face, the same soothing presence — and everything subsided into a wave of bliss, more ecstasy than I had ever experienced. After the course, for a while, I had to get used to my new bearings. I plunged myself into Art of Living activities, went for *satsangs* every Thursday and generally found myself happier than ever before.

"Then the great day came, Gurudev was to pass through Mumbai on the way to Bangalore. A *satsang* was organized and I found myself helping in the preparation. Soon it was time and the *satsang* started. Eagerly we awaited the arrival of the guru. At that time, Khurshed, my teacher, asked me to go and man the Divine Shop that was at the entrance of the hall. This meant I couldn't participate in the *satsang* to my heart's content. I was dejected a trifle, as I felt I wouldn't see the Guru. But that night after the *satsang*, some of us assembled in Sangita Jani's house, where Gurudev was resting for the night. As the night progressed, he sent everyone out and finally only two of us, Harish and myself, were left. At that time, I realized that whatever effort (!) I put into helping, it was always rewarded way beyond my imagination.

"Just two months after the Basic Course, I got to know about an Advanced Course in the *ashram* at Bangalore. Notwithstanding the fact that it was in the middle of the semester, I just talked to my professors and went to participate in the course. Landing in Bangalore, we hitchhiked to the *ashram* in a passing vehicle, and finally I was home. The *satsang* and the silence were awesome. And, on the second day of the Advanced Course, in this perfect setting, Sri Sri walked into the session — majestic, yet subtle, followed by a tumult of emotions, yet serene, an embodiment of silence and love. In the silence I could feel his presence spread as a vast effulgence of grace. And permeating each and every cell of creation, he stood there smiling — it seemed only for me.

"One experience stands out. It was an hour-long meditation and at the start, Gurudev instructed us to remain perfectly still. I was sitting in the aisle, and after the meditation started, I felt ants crawling all over the body. Dismissing it as an experience in the meditation, I continued to stay still. However as the meditation proceeded, my whole body was covered in red ants, biting all over the place. However, I still adhered to Gurudev's instruction. Sit still I did, and by the end of the meditation, I had experienced a catharsis beyond description. It was as if he stood by my side helping me through the process. That was when I realized that every experience is just a tool for the guru to open me up, more and more.

"During my first *Navaratri* at the *ashram*, I experienced a whole new aspect of my beloved Gurudev. This was the first time I had observed the total silence — a silence that encompassed the surroundings, people and events. In the midst of the sound of Vedic chanting, the clang of the cymbals and the beat of the drums, Sri Sri sat unmoved, untouched and yet totally immersed in all the happenings. Without uttering a word, without moving a muscle, he seemed to be doing everything."

Another of our friends, who prefers to remain anonymous, had this story to tell: "I was new to the Art of Living and, during an Advanced Course, I had given rather a tart reply to Gurudev — and then immediately regretted it. By the time we all retired for the night, my remorse had reached such intensity that I sat in my room crying bitterly for a couple of hours. I was inconsolable. In the morning, our course leader told us that the previous night Gurudev had been concerned about a woman who had cried in her room for a long time. The course leader went on and explained that Gurudev had asked him to deliver a message to all of us, but especially to the lady who had been crying; 'Let go of each moment as it passes. Forgive others, but especially yourself. Let go of all judgements and blame and learn to perceive and honour the Divine who dwells in yourself, as well as in others.

The Divine is free of all blame and that is how we all are at the core of our being.' I felt such a sweetness in my heart, that not only was Gurudev not offended or angry with me, but that he was concerned about my distress. Later on, I heard Gurudev say, 'Remember the guru does not hold faults and weaknesses against you. The guru has come to help you with these faults.' "

A fashion designer by profession, Hima Parikh had dabbled in fabrics and was struggling to keep up a strained marital life till she did the Basic Course: "Before the Basic Course, I designed clothes — but never had thought that I could design my life. My approach to life was very materialistic and there was no joy in it. I was so lonely. I began to sense that I could not handle my child, my house, my family or my business. At this point my husband suggested that we should separate because our relationship was also deteriorating. But that same month, we took the Basic Course together, and immediately felt a connection in our hearts that had been lacking in the three years of our married life. Thanks to the *Sudarshan Kriya*, my life changed totally and thanks to this powerful breathing practice my depression and tensions disappeared and for the first time *param shanti* and *param anand* (supreme peace and supreme happiness) became more than just words to me. Even before the course was over, I started perceiving the problems and situations in my life in a more positive manner. Soon I went to the Bangalore *ashram* for the Advanced Course, but it was really just an excuse to meet Gurudev. The *ashram* felt like home. Every moment spent with Gurudev was filled with joy, knowledge and love. His playfulness provokes laughter but, even in his mischief, there is profound wisdom." The list of such stories is endless.

CHAPTER TEN

THE
MIRACLES

In science knowledge comes first and then
  faith follows.
In spirituality faith comes first and then
  knowledge follows.

*W*ESTERNERS ARE PARTICULARLY WARY OF "MIRACLES", although Christ is supposed to have performed many. I am uneasy, for instance, when I read the life of Sai Baba and hear of him appearing in three different places at the same time when he was young. Yet, the one time I met Sai Baba, I definitely felt "something" as I witnessed him materialize "*vibhuti*". I have also talked to some of his disciples — intelligent, coherent, serious men and women — who told me they had seen him with their own eyes changing a stone into a diamond, or silver into gold. So I give gurus the benefit of the doubt that they must be capable of performing miracles, although the Cartesian streak in me still has qualms about it. For me the greatest of miracles that a guru can perform is to change his disciples' natures, a near impossible task. Nevbertheless, a book about Sri Sri cannot skip the subject of miracles, as it is the most common refrain of his disciples: "Guru*ji* performed this miracle or that miracle on me"; "I couldn't walk, I walked"; "I had cancer, I got cured"; "I was blind, I saw." We have now met so many good, serious and truthful teachers and disciples of AOL, who have told us about the miracles which happened to them. Having observed Sri Sri for about seven years now, for me the greatest of miracles is the smile and energy that manifests in people through his presence.

On the final day of one of the Advanced Courses we attended, in the experience sharing session, a number of people came on stage to recount their miraculous experiences.

Shyam Sunder Sardana, an industrialist from Haryana reported a remarkable recovery from a near-fatal heart condition. "I had been a heart patient since my forties. With my angina I had to take precautions due to high blood pressure and hypertension. I had a heart attack at forty-eight, and had been on heavy medication since. I had my first heart surgery at fifty-six when I was diagnosed as having blocked arteries. In February of 1998, when I had aggravated breathing problems I went for a detailed check up. Tests showed that I was just on the brink of death. All the physicians gave me a maximum of six months to live. I was advised not to climb stairs, nor to leave the room. I would feel breathlessness and could hardly walk fifteen hundred yards.

"In May of 1999 during this bedridden condition, I read about the Basic Course in the Sunday news magazine and on Monday, I contacted the Art of Living teacher, Nityanand. I told him of my problem, and took the Basic Course the next week. After the course, there was a sea change in my condition. I could move about and my health improved considerably. In July, I went to the doctor to see if I could travel to Rishikesh to take an Advanced Course. When I was examined, the doctor was astonished. He asked me, 'Is this the same heart I examined last month?' And I told him, 'Yes, but there's a little change. I have switched over to *Sudarshan Kriya* in addition to the pills from you!' He had a good laugh. By the time I met Gurudev and did the Advanced Course, I was fully back in shape. Up till now I have had no problems. I have travelled to Germany and walked up snow clad mountain slopes. I, who was given just six months to live, and that too as a vegetable in bed, am now hale and hearty and have lived a normal life for the last three years, by the grace of the guru."

Namrita's roommate, Dr. Ramola Prabhu had a different story to share. "The phone rang at four in the morning in New York. It was a nurse from the Shock Trauma Unit in Maryland. Our son had just had surgery for a deep laceration in his right temple. We stood trembling and unbelieving as the chief nurse reassured us that we were very lucky parents and could now take our son back home. My husband, Ganesh, and our two daughters rushed to Maryland, while I stayed behind in New York. The same afternoon that Gokul returned home from the hospital, Gurudev arrived in New York.

Amazingly, the people who were supposed to pick him up arrived much later and I found myself alone with him at the airport, just as the heart had desired. Groping for words to tell him, before I could utter anything, I heard him say, 'Gokul had an accident, didn't he? Don't worry, he will be okay.' Unashamedly, and unabated, I let the tears of gratitude flow! What Gokul related to me when I got back home, was nothing short of a miracle. It was dark and, trying to avoid another car driving towards him in the wrong lane, he hit a lamppost. His right side was soaked in blood and each time he tried to stand up, he fainted. Out of nowhere, a 'man' appeared from the darkness and asked Gokul if he needed help. No car, no light, no other sound, just this man offering to help. Soon the police arrived and Gokul was flown by helicopter to the Shock Trauma Center. I called the police station the next day, wanting to thank the person who had brought help and saved my son. The answer I got was amazing; — 'There is no record of anyone calling.' Who was this man in the darkness who helped Gokul?"

Snjezana Nisevic, an AOL teacher from Croatia, recounted the story of Nexhmedin, "We started to spread Guru*ji*'s knowledge in Kosovo immediately after the war. It was hard and wonderful work and one would often have to stick AOL posters on tanks. Kosovo is inhabited by orthodox Muslims who are closed to new knowledge, and at the same time are wonderful, hospitable, and full of grateful-ness and respect for this knowledge, as soon as they open-up. Nexhmedin, for instance, was a twenty-six-year-old man from Kosovo. He is married and has a small son. The beginning of all the wars in Balkan found him in the Serbian army fighting against the Croats. From that army, he ran away to Bosnia where he joined the Muslim army. There he went through the worst moments of his life, lying in a mass grave among dead bodies. From that place, he ran away to Kosovo and joined the Kosovo army in war against the Serbian army. When the war ended, Nexhmedin wandered in the mountains on the border with Albania completely lost and unable to return to his family and resume normal life. He was wounded in his spine and unable to walk without crutches. However, the most serious consequence he was suffering from was a heavy form of PTSD (Post Traumatic Stress Disorder) manifested as epileptic attacks several times per day, long periods of amnesia and loss of consciousness. When he finally returned home, his family was desperate because of his condition.

"We persuaded him to do the AOL Basic Course. During the course, Nexhmedin felt so much better that he travelled to another city with teachers and went through the Basic Course once again. After the course, all the PTSD symptoms disappeared! There were no more epileptic attacks, amnesia or loss of consciousness! And all this in a period of two weeks! After one month, Nexhmedin came to learn *Sahaj Samadhi* meditation! With a smile on his face, he said that he had been doing the programme regularly and that he did not need crutches any longer! Now he has a great desire to meet Guru*ji*."

With some prodding, Vasanthi Narayanan, our Advanced Course teacher, told us her miraculous story. "I came in contact with Guru*ji* around 1988. At the time I was suffering from numerous health problems, spinal problems and spondilitis with a lot of breathing difficulties. The doctors had given me only six months to live as all these were putting pressure on my heart. I was in a depressed state of mind and the family also reflected this as they were worried about me. I used to pray to Krishna everyday. One day, I sat and prayed that he take me today — I didn't even want to live the six months given to me. While I was praying, I had a vision. It was as if it had rained and I saw a ten-year-old boy, dressed in white like Krishna, stretching out his hand to me. I was down in a deep dark well and he asked me to take his hand to come up. As I tried to hold his hand, he just picked me up in his arms and brought me up. That energy and that light gave me a wonderful warmth inside me and I thought God had taken me already. After an hour or two I opened my eyes and realized that I was still in this world.

"Within two days of this experience there was a *satsang* in the house of somebody working in the Indian High Commission in Singapore to which I was invited. When I got there it was as if they were waiting for someone, some yogi. I did not want to talk to anybody.

The door opened and suddenly Gurudev came in and I felt 'How come? Yesterday you were within me and today you are here.' I felt this emptiness in me. I did not have any other thought other than "Here is my Krishna." I decided to do the the Basic Course which was very painful and difficult, but after some time I felt very good and perceived that the whole body had changed. I removed my lumbar belt, my collar and I could BREATHE. Soon after that I came to the *ashram*, in Bangalore, and stayed for nineteen days. With Guru*ji*'s grace I was completely cured during this time and I went back a new person, with renewed energy. I was fulfilled. It was not the old Vasanthi, on the mental or any other level. This was a real miracle for me. Before coming in contact with Gurudev, I was a very reserved person and would not meet many people. Now I travel all over the world to teach courses. And it is quite amazing how I meet people and feel at home everywhere. I feel guided wherever I go and know I am taken care of."

It was then the turn of Eva Lewarne, an American, who is no novice to spiritual life, having been a student of a Tibetan Buddhist Lama for nine years, to come on the stage: "I first met him when I went to attend a public talk given by him in Toronto. Although I was reluctant to go, once there, I experienced one of the most profound moments of my life! As soon as I sat down in the auditorium, I felt bathed in an atmosphere of joy, peace and incredible love, which intensified when he walked in and all I could do was sit in meditative bliss. The room seemed to fill with the most amazing perfume and there was such a profound feeling, which I shared with my friend, 'Here is a man whose feet I could sit at for the rest of my life!' I felt totally relaxed, irrespective of the fact that I had recently been diagnosed with cancer of the ovaries at Princess Margaret Hospital and the doctor felt the need for a quick date for the operation, as soon as he got the result of a particular blood test. But right now, I was totally oblivious to everything else and loved the way Guruji spontaneously answered the numerous questions put to him. I felt reluctant to leave, and hung around in the hope that he might walk by me. To my amazement he did, and the thought flashed that if I touched him, I would be healed. I touched him. And, to cut a long story short, I went back to the hospital the following Tuesday and heard from my doctor that I was a very baffling case — my blood test came back negative! Saying thank you seems very insignificant in the face of the miracle Guruji performed on me."

Our friend Raghu Raj Raja, whom Gurudev once sent to Japan to conduct Art of Living Courses, recounted this story: "A twenty-three-year-old girl named Yako, who had an accident when she was sixteen, was brought to one of the courses. She was in a wheel chair, unable to walk or even lift her hands. Yako and her mother had come with tremendous hope. They were tired of all the medications that had been prescribed over the years. Though I doubted whether she could handle the course, I allowed Yako to sit through the first day of instruction.

That night, Gurudev telephoned me from Germany, and even before I could begin, he said, 'Doesn't matter even if the *pranayama* positions are not all right, she can still do the *Kriya*.' After the first *Sudarshan Kriya*, Yako found that she could lift her hands and bring them down at will. After the second *Kriya*, she could actually walk, with a bit of help. The girl and her mother were overwhelmed. Tears of gratitude flowed from their eyes, and they wished to take the first opportunity to meet Gurudev. Yako's experience was aired on Tokyo Radio, which inspired numerous people to join the Art of Living."

Dr. Saran, a paediatrician from Mongolia, who has travelled around the world with her husband who is a top official with WHO, had this to say: "When Guru*ji* was in Ulaan Bator, on a state visit in April this year, we were amazed at the devotion and connectedness of the Mongolian people, most of whom were seeing him for the first time. Heads bowed and eyes filled with tears, they came in hundreds to have a glimpse of the 'Living God' as they addressed him. In the crowd was a lady who had been paralysed and bedridden for years. When she saw Guru*ji*'s photo in the newspaper, she immediately recognized him as her guru, rose from her bed and walked to the *satsang* for his *darshan*, where she shared her healing experience, as we looked on in wonder."

Sangeeta Jani still remembers when her apartment caught fire: "Usually at around 7.00 p.m. I take a shower and meditate but, on this particular day, a friend of mine coaxed me to go out with her. While I was out, I felt very restless. On reaching home, I found the whole building in darkness and water all around. My neighbours rushed to tell me that my entire floor had caught fire and everything had been destroyed. For a couple of minutes, I couldn't register what they were saying. When I went upstairs, I was shocked to see the state of my apartment. Everything seemed to be destroyed. Then, through the shambles, I saw my altar still covered with silk, adorned by Gurudev's *padukas*. A short circuit had occurred and all that remained were the altar and my Art of Living papers. Not even a toothbrush had been spared; even an audiocassette lying on top of a *satsang* book got burnt, but the book survived not only the fire, but also the water from the fire brigade rescue team. If I had taken my shower according to routine, I would have been trapped. With the guru's grace, guidance came in the form of my friend!"

Dr. Ramola Prabhu shared with us another inspiring healing experience: "A few years ago my aunt was diagnosed with an undifferentiated, very malignant meta-static tumor in the neck. The doctors did not know where the primary site was, and so my aunt suffered the ravages of full body radiation and chemotherapy. Given less than six months to live, my uncle and aunt decided to spend some time with their grandchildren in Europe, as their son was settled there. We convinced them to visit us in the US. Their itinerary changed and they arrived in Baltimore. Coincidentally, the same weekend a Basic Course was happening in our home. Throughout the

Sudarshan Kriya, my aunt complained of a severe burning sensation in her neck, but somehow she completed the course. Shortly thereafter they returned to India. It is now almost seven years since my aunt was told she had six months to live. She regularly practises the *Kriya*, is very much alive and completely healthy. Currently she runs a school for the underprivileged children of her area."

M., an English lady, concluded the session by recollecting her story: "Two years ago, I needed surgery to remove my uterus. The doctor was not competent enough and made a mistake. He damaged the wall of my bladder and that affected my kidney. After the surgery my abdominal pain remained, and in the next three months it worsened. I decided to come to India for better medical treatment. A scan showed a foreign body lodged in my abdomen, a small clip left behind by the surgeon in the previous operation! The doctors here decided to perform another surgery to remove the object. I decided to wait till Guru*ji*'s return from Germany and have his *darshan* before going ahead with the operation. As the pain grew worse, and based on the doctors' prognosis, I resigned myself to the surgery. I spoke to Gurudev over the telephone and he asked me to do a meditation. On the seventh morning I had to go for a preoperative scan. The next morning, Guru*ji* arrived and I went for a *puja* at the *ashram* before going to collect the report. When I reached the medical centre, I found the doctors were incredulous; there was no trace of the object. The clip had completely disappeared!"

The experiences I had heard about were truly breathtaking for me, and I decided to ask Sri Sri about them, during our next meeting: "What do you think about all these healing experiences and miracles?" He smiled and answered, "Life is a mystery. It has to be lived, not understood." I left his cottage, not entirely clear what he meant, yet beginning to ponder on the answer.

I went back to my room, which I shared with S B Ganguly, an industrialist from Calcutta. He also had his own story to tell! One early morning, when Ganguly went for a walk from his house in upmarket Kolkata, he was kidnapped and taken to a remote place. The kidnappers were hardened criminals, and they demanded a fat ransom. The news made headlines. Ganguly was a prominent industrialist in Kolkata. Kept in a dark room for many days, he prayed intensely to Guru*ji* during that period. Throughout the nightmare, Ganguly distinctly heard Guru*ji*'s voice, assuring him, "I am with you and nothing will happen to you." After some time, suddenly Ganguly noticed a drastic change in the attitude of the terrorists, who started taking care of him, feeding him, and even providing him with his daily diabetic pills! Soon, without making any demands, they released S B Ganguly, with a note of apology for the inconvenience!!

As Ganguly finished the story, Sanjeev who was quietly observing us talking, showed me a letter from Cathy Champion in St. Louis, reporting a curious incident that occurred to her husband, which was reproduced in *An Intimate Note to the Sincere Seeker*. When Cathy's husband

Mike, a fitness freak who never missed work, suddenly complained about his pain in shoulder, she knew it was something serious. The MRI showed damage to nerves and muscles; the diagnosis after the X-rays was a torn rotator cuff, and surgery was scheduled. When Cathy received a flier for a talk by Sri Sri scheduled the day before the surgery, she and Mike thought it was a good way to spend the evening. At the talk, Cathy found Sri Sri's voice and his persona strangely familiar. At the end of the talk, they decided to stand in a three-hundred-people long queue to meet Sri Sri, which was quite unusual for them. When their turn came, Cathy found herself asking for Mike's safety during the next day's surgery. Sri Sri called for a rose and handed it to Mike, advising him to keep the rose by his side, and assuring him that "all will be well". And so it was.

Finally, Rajshree shared her amazing story: The very day she landed at Bangalore from Gujarat, Sri Sri asked her to go to Mumbai, saying, "You will have a blast!" Reluctantly, Rajshree went to Mumbai, and organized a course in Chembur, an area quite a distance away from where she lived. On the second day of the course, the famous Bombay bomb blasts took place, following which riots ensued. The areas that Rajshree had to cross to go to the course venue were among the most sensitive and riot-prone. There was a limited curfew in effect. Determined to keep her commitment to the course, Rajshree persuaded a taxi to take her to Chembur, and miraculously, the taxi reached her to the venue safely, amidst looting, arson and dacoity! After returning from the course, Rajshree found the phone ringing and Sri Sri joking, "I told you, you would have a blast!"

Sri Sri was scheduled to transit through Mumbai the next day from Germany, and Rajshree tried to persuade him to take a flight via Delhi or Chennai for security reasons. He refused and gave her the flight details, but Rajshree was unsure if she would be able to make it to the airport due to the curfew. On the next day of the course, all sixty participants were in attendance as it was a gated colony. One of the participants asked her permission to leave the course early, which she refused. At the end of that session, a lady invited her to have tea at her home. As Rajshree was walking there, she noticed the same gentleman who sought her permission to leave the course early, entering a house marked Commissioner of Police. Rajshree remarked that it was a good tactic to keep the intruders away! The lady laughed, saying that the man was indeed the Commissioner of Police, and that he had sought permission to leave the course early due to the curfew! When Rajshree told her that she had to start for the airport to receive Guru*ji*, the Commissioner volunteered to drive her, saying that it would otherwise be impossible for her to reach otherwise, as "shoot at sight" orders were imposed in the area. Just as both of them reached the airport in the car of the Commissioner of Police, Sri Sri arrived at the gate, and remarked, "See, I told you, you would find a way!"

The more I think about all these experiences, the more

Sri Sri's words echo in my mind, "Life is a mystery. It has to be lived, not understood."

CHAPTER ELEVEN

THE SEARCH FOR
SCIENTIFIC PROOF

"Life without wisdom is incomplete,

Wisdom that does not give rise to feelings
is incomplete,

Feeling that does not transfer into action
is incomplete,

Action that does not give rise to fulfillment
is incomplete,

Fulfillment is returning to self."

I HAVE NOW BEEN WITH THE ART OF LIVING LONG ENOUGH to recognize the authenticity of the claims of healing experiences made by people around me. After all, my own breathing disorders healed dramatically after the practice of the *Sudarshan Kriya*. Yet, my mind, groomed in western upbringing, needed additional scientific proof. For some time, I wondered why scientific establishments did not take up the active lead in measuring the impact of these practices. The question remained with me, until I received an invitation to attend the "Science of Breath" symposium from the All India Institute of Medical Sciences (AIIMS). I happened to be in Delhi at that time, and visited the conference a couple of times — I could sense that the results were dramatic, though could not understand the medical jargon. This is my understanding of what science has proved. Basically, there have been four major findings on the impact of *Sudarshan Kriya* and related breathing practices taught in the Art of Living Course:

The All India Institute of Medical Sciences has taken EEG pictures of the brain, reproduced here. The change in colour from blue to yellowish red indicates "high beta wave activity" which means greater integration of the left (logical) and right (aesthetic) hemispheres of the brain, and improved awareness. This shows that the person's mind is in a state of "relaxed wakefulness" and "heightened awareness".

Dr Geeta of Bangalore University presented a paper on the capability of the *Sudarshan Kriya* to treat depression — seventy per cent of the people who practised it overcame it. The practice was as effective as popular drugs, without the dependence or side effects.

Studies have also shown that *Sudarshan Kriya* is an effective stress-buster. Proxies of stress such as the Stress Hormone (Serum Cortisol) and Stress Enzyme (Serum Lactose) show a marked decrease after the practice, indicating a relaxation response. Doctors surmise that the glucose spared from the muscles and RBCs during the practice are made available to the brain, leading to a state of body relaxation and mental alertness. This study also showed that the Serum Cortisol levels of Art of Living teachers was dramatically low, probably due to the regularity of practice, and the impact of Advanced programmes.

Of some interest to the medical community is also the dramatic increase in natural killer cells in cancer patients and increase in good cholesterol simultaneously with the reduction in bad cholesterol in the system. Are these metabolic changes the reason why *Sudarshan Kriya* is able to heal a wide array of diseases? When I asked this question to Dr. Manikantan, the Ayurvedic teacher at Bangalore *ashram*, he said, "When the balance of the *doshas* is restored in the system, diseases automatically cure." Sri Sri, on different occasions has remarked about the need to attend to health. "Half the health we spend gaining our wealth," he says, "and then spend half our wealth trying to gain back our health — this is not a very intelligent thing to do."

The following are some of the medical courses offered by AOL.

Medical Courses

AOL courses are not only meant as a psychological tool to feel better and lead a more harmonious life, they are also extremely efficient in treating psychiatric, psychological, social and medical problems, which have often left modern medicine baffled. Depression, for instance, is a disabling disease that takes the joy out of life for millions around the world — men, women, and children — regardless of race, income, or family background. It also contributes, remarks Sri Sri, "to the downward spiral of many diseases, from cancer and HIV to asthma and cardiovascular disease. Finding an effective treatment for depression is a global health concern." The Art of Living Course for Depression offers a variety of techniques that have been documented by independent medical studies to be effective in alleviating dejection. These simple, yet powerful techniques have advantages over many other forms of treatment because they are free from negative side-effects, cut health care costs, and are easy to learn and practise in daily life.

However, due to the often long-term and chronic nature of depression, Art of Living Courses for Depression usually run longer than regular Art of Living Course and are sometimes taught as in-residence programmes.

Many of us, as we age, incur the risk of Coronary Heart Disease (CHD). In fact, anyone can develop CHD regardless of age, sex, race or ethnic backgrounds. Sometimes there may be no warning signs and symptoms and even if there are any, either they are not noticed or they are ignored. The history of CHD is higher in urban population than in the rural, which is a major cause for premature death. When three risk factors like hyper-Lipidemia (high fat and cholesterol content in blood), hypertension and smoking are present in an individual, the chances of a heart attack is seven times higher whereas, when individually present the risk is two-fold. Whatever may be the risk factor, the basic pathology of CHD is deposition of LDL Cholesterol (Harmful Cholesterol), fat and other substances on the walls of the coronary arteries. These deposits thicken the arterial walls and narrow the arteries, which slows or blocks the flow of blood. The heart receives a constant supply of oxygen through blood, any blockage of which may result in chest pain (angina pectoris) and myocardial infoction (heart attack) or even death.

It is my experience, as an ex-smoker and a sportsman, that regular *Sudarshan Kriya* practice, *Ujjai*, *Pranayama*, and *Bhastrika* can work wonders: one has a better all round general health, more stamina, more lung capacity and even the eyesight improves. My humble findings seem to have a medical sanction: the All India Medical Institute conducted a study on forty-six normal participants, whose lipid profile which involves study of serum cholestrol (Total), HDLc (good Cholesterol), LDLc (harmful Cholesterol) and triglycerides were analysed before the start of *Sudarshan Kriya* practice and consecutively on the seventh and forty-fifth day after regular *Sudarshan Kriya* practice. Amazingly, there was a statistically significant decrease in serum total cholesterol, LDL cholesterol (harmful) and lipid peroxidation, and an increase in HDL cholesterol (good). The hypocholestrimic action of *Sudarshan Kriya* practice suggests being a tool for the prevention of a deranged lipid profile and hypertension, which is a major risk factor for CHD. Which, put in plain language, means that if you practise *Sudarshan Kriya*, you run five times less chance of suffering a heart attack after fifty.

One morning Namrita and I were sipping our tea on the veranda, when Radha our maidservant, arrived weeping, totally shattered about her husband Raju's habit of heavy drinking. He had come home totally drunk the night before, beat her up, slapped the children and then collapsed in a drunken stupor. Seeing her pain and anguish, we went and met a sorrowful Raju a little later. We reached out to him, talked to him and convinced him to do the Art of Living Course for alcoholics.

All of us have felt, at one time or the other, the urge to indulge in mood elevating experiences, such as alcohol, grass, or even stronger hallucinogenic stuff. Alcohol seems to be, not only in the west, but also unfortunately in India, the one socially accepted custom. But sadly, the repeated consumption of alcoholic beverages ultimately leads to a dreadful dependence, wherein one needs to drink more and more to get the same pleasurable experience. And anyone who has tried to sever the habit, must have gone through very unpleasant withdrawal symptoms. In one word: Alcoholism is a dreadful disease which is creating havoc in the world not only on people's wallets, but on their mind and on their health. Here are a few statistics to prove my point: In 1976, liquor manufacturers in India utilized 169.4 million litres of absolute alcohol, enough to manufacture 350 million bottles of rum. The absolute alcohol used by manufacturers rose to 207.9 million litres in 1981, 331 million litres in 1985, 459 million litres in 1991 and 700 million litres in 2001.

This high proportion of problem-drinkers in India has led to more frequent health visits at hospitals and clinics due to alcohol related illnesses. The studies done at a large general hospital in Bangalore revealed that 40 per cent of all males and 6.6 per cent of all females admitted for medical and surgical problems, had a drinking problem. Many treatment approaches have been used to treat alcoholism all over the world, such as pharmacological therapy, disulfiram therapy, aversion therapy and non-pharmacological therapy (alcohol anonymous, psychotherapy, relapse therapy, etc). While each of these treatments has met with limited success in achieving abstinence, the pharmacological treatment appears to be more promising in the management of alcoholism. But still, the rate of relapse is in the region of forty to fifty per cent. Here comes Sri Sri's all round *Sudarshan Kriya*, which was tested in 1999 in the NIMHANS medical institute of Bangalore on sixty heavily alcohol-dependent men, willing to stay closeted for three weeks .The patients were first allowed to detoxify for seven days. Once the detoxification completed, the patients were randomly allocated into two treatment groups of equal size having thirty patients for each group for thirty days. Group 1 received only the standard treatment: family therapy, psychotherapy,and diazepam was also prescribed for up to six months after the three weeks of treatment. Group 2 was made to go into silence and practise *yoga asanas*, *pranayama* and *Sudarshana Kriya* under supervision. After twenty-five days, it was observed that all those alcoholics practising *Sudarshana Kriya* showed improvement physically and psychologically and are now living without relapse, while seventy-five per cent of Group 1 relapsed within six months. Raju was one of the lucky ones and has stayed clean for many years. Radha's smile says it all.

The most dreadful disease of modern times is of course cancer, which has touched all of us in some manner: a mother, a father, a cherished uncle, a brother maybe, slowly wasting away before our horrified eyes. Diagnosis of cancer is a challenging and stressful situation in anyone's life. And even though cancer is more survivable than ever before, coping with cancer can take a heavy physical, mental and emotional toll. Mounting scientific data suggests that immune system function, quality, and even the very length of life are all profoundly impacted by one's mental and emotional state. Healing and resistance to disease are not simply functions of the body — one's state of mind and emotions significantly affect physical health. Whether you are dealing with the side effects of cancer treatment, or the emotional upheaval of a recent cancer diagnosis, Art of Living Cancer Courses offer a wealth of practical techniques and knowledge that promote health on every level. They feature of course the *Sudarshan Kriya* technique, which supports the healing process by reducing the effects of stress, restoring vital energy, and by enabling one to get a better night's sleep. It also plays a vital role in how effectively the mind, body and emotions interact to create health.

We not only live in a world of stress, but many people encounter traumatic situations which leave terrible after-effects: wars, earthquakes, rapes, road accidents. To help these trauma victims regain their centre through the different *pranayama* techniques has proved very beneficial. AOL volunteers have for example worked with trauma victims of the 2001 earthquake in Gujarat, India, and in the war torn Balkans. The effectiveness of *Sudarshan Kriya* and the other breathing exercises on trauma survivors have also been conducted at the National Institute of Mental Health and Neurosciences (NIMHANS) of India, the premiere institute for the study of neuroscience and mental health. It has been found (see charts in the Appendix) that the levels of cortisol, decreased significantly in subjects who practised *Sudarshana Kriya* within twenty-one days. NIMHANS research has also documented accelerated neuronal processing of, and recovery from stressful stimuli. This means the brain more quickly returns to normal after receiving stressful stimuli.

Additionally, sleep disturbances (measured in depressed populations), normalized improving both the length and quality of sleep.

Another pilot study of persons under trauma shock conducted by the Institute for Rehabilitation of the Republic of Slovenia documented significant reductions in anxiety levels (as measured by the widely used STAI) within five days of learning *Sudarshana Kriya* and significant increases in alpha activity and in plasma prolactin, which also is believed to produce feelings of well-being. It was also found that it induced high frequency

EEG activity, which is indicative of greater concentration and mental focus.

Ayurveda

Sri Sri Ravi Shankar is a champion of the renaissance of Ayurveda, because he feels that many of today's so-called incurable diseases can be treated by this form of medication, which has been thoroughly tried and tested, and can be used very effectively to treat all kinds of disorders. What is Ayurveda ? It is the science of restoring balance in an individual on a physical, psychological, and spiritual level: ayur (of life)-veda (science) uses herbs, diet, lifestyle, yoga, vedic astrology, color therapy, energy-points (using pressure, puncture, heat and oils), aroma-therapy, gemstones, *vastu shastra* (similar to Feng Shui), and various other therapeutic means to promote well being — *Sukham.*

"The unique constitutions of our body/mind/sense complexes with which we are born move out of balance by inappropriate diet and lifestyles, as well as unresolved emotions," says Sri Sri Ravi Shankar. "These imbalances eventually progress into disease. Ayurvedic medicine recognizes and treats a traditional seven stage patho-genesis, only the last two obvious stages of which, disease and deformity, are usually diagnosed and treated in western medicine."

As in medical traditions from Persia to China, and elsewhere, "Pulse Diagnosis" is used in Ayurvedic medicine as a principal diagnostic tool to read a person's present and past physical and mental health. By understanding and applying what it means to actively live in harmony with universal laws that influence our existence, Ayurveda guides us in healing, preventing disorders, rejuvenating, and revitalizing ourselves on the physical, psychological, and spiritual levels.

In Ayurveda every individual has a unique combination of physical, mental and emotional characteristics. Body, mind and consciousness work together in maintaining balance. Internal and external factors can act to disturb one's balance, and both physical and mental disturbances are reflected through the skin. Also, the Ayurvedic system recognizes that both the environment and human beings are composed of five basic elements: air, space, fire, water and earth. The predominance of these elements affects the three metabolic characteristics of individuals, referred to as *doshas*. These three *doshas* are *vata*, *pitta* and *kapha*, and individuals can be classified as one of these three constitutions or as a combination of two or even three of the *doshas*.

The goal of Ayurvedic Healthcare Products and Services is to help individuals take advantage of the strengths of their *doshas* while at the same time limiting the weaknesses. This is made possible by maintaining the *doshas* at an optimal level through a range of treatments gathered in Ayurvedic texts.

The Art of Living Foundation has a dispensary which manufactures a growing variety of Ayurvedic products, which are meant to maintain and/or enhance general health, prevent imbalance, cleanse tissues and purge toxins. They are not claimed to cure any doctor-defined disease. In no case do AOL doctors recommend or prescribe herbs, nor do they diagnose, treat, prevent or cure disease. On the contrary, they will advise you to always consult a qualified physician for any medical condition.

Here are a few sample medicines: *Makardhwaj*, is a general tonic and a traditional Ayurvedic male aphrodisiac. *Shatavari* (asparagus raceosus) is the main rejuvenative herb for the female, as *Ashwagandha* is for the male. *Shatavari* nourishes and cleanses the blood and the female reproductive organs. It is particularly useful for women who are nursing as well as during menopause, and specially for those who have undergone a hysterectomy operation. *Shilajit* (asphaltum) is a general rejuvenator that promotes strength and immunity and is also used to support the proper function of urinary tract and prostate. It also reduces excess *kapha*. *Triphla*, detoxifies and rejuvenates. This formulation is a *tri-doshic* Ayurvedic formula. It is used as mild laxative and can be taken both for preventive and curative purposes. It strengthens the digestion and improves eye vision, and is beneficial for liver problems and hair loss. It is also used to support weight management and improve the complexion. *Triphla Guggul*, minimizes the accumulation of toxins in the GI tract and joints, and supports proper digestion and elimination. It decongests the body channels, removes toxins from the tissues, rekindles the digestive fire and promotes healthy metabolism. It also removes excess *kapha* from the body.

In India every third shop is an allopathic pharmacy selling drugs made by multinationals, which sometimes do more harm than good. Antibiotics, for instance, not only kill the microbes but also the good elements in our body, whereas *neem*, only destroys the harmful bugs (*neem* is *shakti* says Guruji). It is high time that India rediscovers the wonder that is Ayurveda, the oldest medical system of the world still in practice.

CHAPTER TWELVE

SRI SRI'S ANSWERS
FOR THE WORLD TODAY

The self knows neither sorrow nor death, yet in it flow all relative events. It is easy to be detached when you are not in love. Being in utter love and yet undisturbed, caring yet not worried, persistent yet not perturbed — all are the obvious signs of self shining through.

OVER THE LAST FEW YEARS OF ASSOCIATION WITH SRI Sri, I have seen how his model of social reform contains many answers that the world is searching for today. Perhaps that is why increasingly Sri Sri and other teachers are invited to talk on a range of issues in many diverse forms. I have found many of Sri Sri's perspectives to be of immense value in understanding and addressing the core of 21st century issues of terrorism, religion and education. Here are my compilations of some of Sri Sri's Question and Answer sessions.

Terrorism

I heard from John Osborne about a curious encounter that Sri Sri had with a fanatic, at a public talk in

Washington, USA. A tall, well-built man who was sitting at the back of the hall suddenly walked to the stage, yelling and gesticulating at Sri Sri. As he approached within striking distance, raising his hands as if to strangle Sri Sri, the three-hundred-strong audience sat frozen with shock. As he looked into Sri Sri's eyes, Sri Sri just raised his hand, and said "Wait". None knows what happened. The attacker sat where he was, with tears in his eyes. Someone from the audience took the attacker to the side, and Sri Sri continued the discourse, saying, "It is the ignorance in us that makes us small minded. Fanaticism and rigidity will keep you far away from Divinity. Those who profess fanaticism do not need condemnation but compassion."

Terrorism induces fear and increases poverty, suffering and loss of life with no apparent gain to anyone. Instead of offering or seeking solutions, terrorism looks to destruction as an answer. In acts of terrorism, human values are lost.

Why do people turn to terrorism?

The first factor is frustration and desperation to achieve a goal. When people are desperate to achieve some goal and are unable to do it, the desperation brings up violence in them.

The second factor is belief in a non-verifiable concept of merit and heaven: 'If I die fighting for God, then I will go to heaven, because God wants this act to happen." Who knows? No one can verify these statements.

The third is a staunch belief that "my way is the only way."

The fourth is ignoring human values in order to achieve a goal.

And the fifth is the lack of respect or honour for life itself.

Terrorism is thus based on a concept of God as favouring some and being angry with others. This notion undermines the omnipresence and omnipotence of God. How can an omnipresent God exclude some people? How can an omnipotent God be angry? Anger and frustration arise when someone is unable to do something or control something. With this limited idea of God, you become the saviour of God rather than the servant of God. God is a poor fellow sitting somewhere getting angry, and you are going to help him.

Terrorism fails to recognize that God loves variety and diversity; that many different schools of thought exist in this world. It does not respect or honour life. Terrorism arises when someone identifies himself first and foremost as a member of particular religion, and then is ready to give up his life for that limited identity. We need first to identify ourselves as part of the Divine and second to that, as human beings.

Q: What is the remedy for terrorism?

Sri Sri: As long as there is limited understanding, limited wisdom being imparted in fundamentalist and fanatical schools, there is no way we can rid this world of terrorism.

We have to broaden our vision and educate people about all the different religions and cultural traditions of the world. Religious and spiritual leaders, in particular, should have a broad understanding of cultures and religions. Every *mullah*, every priest and rabbi should know something about all other religions. If we learn to broaden our vision and deepen our roots, people will not fall into a narrow idea of the will of God; They will see life in a broad perspective. It's not just religion that makes people become terrorists, there can be social and political reasons also.

Next, we have to educate people in the human values of friendliness, compassion, cooperation, a sense of belonging and spirituality. We can say that spirituality is that which nourishes the human values of compassion, love, caring, sharing and acceptance. Spirituality is finding a way to calm the mind and go deep in your prayers, irrespective of what prayer you do or what religion you follow. It is honouring the values that are found in all religions. And it is concern for the common good of one and all, accommodating diversity, thought, deed and behaviour in the world.

We have to learn how to cope with the stress of life. Stress and tension are the root cause of violence. Have a sense of belonging to this planet and all its people. Cultivate confidence in achieving a noble goal in a peaceful, non-violent manner. This confidence comes from your inner strength. There are many examples for us of people who have done this: Martin Luther King in the North American continent, Nelson Mandela in the African continent, Mahatma Gandhi in the Asian continent. Only spiritual upliftment can weed out the destructive tendency in the human mind.

Q: Where was God on September 11th?

Sri Sri: Where was God when the Columbine killings occurred? Where was God when the Mississippi River flooded? Where was God when there was a tornado in Florida or the earthquake in Gujarat? Why are you asking only about September 11th? Three hundred and sixty-five days a year calamitous events happen in the world. Whether man-made or natural, calamity is part of life on this planet. We cannot question the existence of Divinity over an event, pleasant or unpleasant. A faith based on God preventing calamities will be weak. Faith is that which stands the test of events. Many of the Christian saints and apostles were persecuted or executed. If they had questioned, "Where is God? Where is God?" faith would have had no place in their lives. Faith is something much bigger, much more fundamental to life than the events that happen throughout life. God is not a toy for your security or a concept for your convenience. God is love. God is the substratum of this universe, the basis of this existence. God is the space in which all things happen.

Q: In the face of such evil, isn't it hard not to question whether there is a God?

Sri Sri: If you have to question whether something is there or not, you must have a concept about it. And if events shake that concept, then the concept will have to change. If you know that God is love and you see that there is love in the world, then you won't question God. But if you think God exists for your security, then when you are in trouble, when you have problems, this question will certainly arise in your mind. And when you have a limited understanding of your life, not knowing that the life energy in you is eternal, is indestructible, is a continuum, then, too, you may question whether there is a God or not. See that God is all-pervading consciousness, that that alone exists, that nothing else exists. You never question whether atoms exist or not; you know atoms exist. That which is the basis of an atom, that field, that space in which everything exists, everything blossoms, grows and perishes, that basic substratum of this creation — let that be your understanding of God. Then you won't ever ask if God exists.

Q: What attitude should we have towards terrorists?

Sri Sri: We need to be compassionate towards terrorists. They are completely mistaken — they are mistaken as to their religious teachings, they have a mistaken idea of freedom, and they are mistaken in what they want to achieve in life because they are inflicting suffering on others and also on themselves. So they need compassion, they need understanding. Directing hatred and anger towards terrorists will not change or improve them. We need to bring transformation in them. For this we need patience, endurance, and compassion.

Q: How can we hope to positively educate a group, like the terrorists, who are so overtly convinced that their way is the only way?

Sri Sri: They do not know that there are other traditions, which also claim to be the only way. Jesus said, "I am the only way." Krishna said, "I am the goal, the only way." The same is said in the Koran and in other scriptures. The purpose of these words is to bring a focus in human awareness, to bring up conviction in a particular moment, to reaffirm one's faith and practices. But these words have been mistaken to be a general statement meaning that this is the only way, to the exclusion of all other paths. They do not say, "Absolutely, this is the only truth that exists," but rather, "Right now, this is the path." This wrong understanding of the verses of scripture has caused upheaval in the minds of many people and is used to justify narrow-mindedness. That is why, again and again, I say we need to emphasize on educating people in all the holy scriptures of the world. Each individual, especially every spiritual and religious leader, should be familiar with all other scriptures and traditions and schools of knowledge in the world.

You accept food and music from every part of the world without reservation, don't you? You don't have to be a Danish to eat Danish pastries or Italian to eat pasta and pizzas. You don't have to be a German to enjoy Beethoven or an Indian to listen to sitar music. Why then, when it comes to wisdom, do we become so narrow-minded? The world would be a poorer place for not knowing the teachings of Buddha who said so much on consciousness and meditation. The world would be a poorer place for not knowing the wisdom of the Upanishads or Jesus' teachings on love or the words of Mohammed and Lao Tzu. When we think that only our own scripture holds truth, then we are nurturing fanaticism.

Terrorists have very narrow vision. What is needed is broader vision and deeper roots. This could bring about harmony and a non-violent attitude in all people. The only way to get rid of fanaticism in the world is broad-based education — multi-cultural, multi-religious education — so that a child growing up does not think that only the Bible or only the Koran holds the truth. Broaden your vision; expand your horizon when it concerns wisdom, faith and education in religious studies. That broader perspective will put an end to the growing fanaticism in the world today.

Q: Your position is that the key response to the situation in the world today is to educate people in human values, and until we have done that in all corners of the world, you say we will not be safe. Is that an achievable goal?

Sri Sri: Definitely! Until a few hundred years ago, there were tribal people who did not wear clothes. Today, in the most remote parts of the world, people wear clothes. People have been educated in understanding numbers, in using electricity, in using a telephone. All the people in the world have been educated in these things. If we can teach people how to count, we can teach them how to live. It is definitely possible. Educating people in human values is not a difficult thing because the values are already present. They are our nature. By nature we are friendly, cooperative, compassionate. If we are unfriendly, it is because of stress and tension. There are meditation and breathing techniques, which can be practised to reduce stress.

Q: What then are the practical steps we can take to lift up human values in the world?

Sri Sri: If a person identifies himself with a race, religion, culture or nationality, that's it! He remains in that position and he will fight for that and die for that and others will die with him. Instead, give him a broader perspective. First and foremost we are part of the Divine. Our second identity is that we are human beings. The third identity we have is that we are male or female. The fourth identity is that we belong to a particular nation. The fifth identity is that we belong to a particular religion. If the right order of identity is understood, then human values are honoured. But if I identify myself with a religion or nationality, forgetting that first I am part of the Divine and that I am a human being, then I bring misery onto myself and onto others also.

Q: If you had the ear of the whole world for one minute, what would your message be?

Sri Sri: Life is sacred. Celebrate life. Care for others and share whatever you have with those less fortunate than you. Broaden your vision, for the whole world belongs to you.

Religions

Religion has three aspects: value, ritual and symbol. The moral and spiritual values are common to all traditions. The symbols and practices, those rituals and customs that form a way of life within a religion, are what distinguish one tradition from another and give each one their charm. The symbols and practices are like the banana skin, and the spiritual values — the quest for truth and knowing deep within us that we are part of divinity — are the banana. People in every tradition have thrown away the banana and are holding onto the skin.

This distinction between value, ritual and symbol was made in ancient times. The Sanskrit term *"smriti"* refers to those practices that are appropriate to a time and place, those things that are time-bound. *"Shruti"* refers to those values which are timeless. And in the right order of things, what is time-bound is secondary to what is timeless or eternal. Putting religious concepts before human values creates havoc. In all traditions, we find the order inverted. People tend to hold what is time-bound — the symbols and practices, those things which give them an individual identity — before the values. Then fanaticism flourishes and the differences have to be defended.

We can see this today in the wars taking place around the world in the name of religion. If we could focus on the values, the larger truth that the symbol represents, then most of the conflict in the world will be resolved.

Symbols vary between religions because they have to do with the relative factors of location, environment and time. The crescent moon and star on the flag of Islam was chosen by people living in a desert region where evening is a pleasant relief from the scorching heat of the day. The sun was chosen as a religious symbol in Japan and in Tibet where it gives welcome warmth and a feeling of elevation. Symbols are relative, but they are intended to lead us to something beyond the symbol, to the essence of religion. We need to reach for the deeper value, not to be stopped by the apparent difference. Practices are also time-bound — how you should dress, what name you are to take, what you can eat, how many wives you may have, how a person should be punished if they make some mistake. In all traditions you find practices like these that were necessary at the time that they were instituted, but they may no longer serve a good purpose today. In the Koran, it is prescribed that if someone steals, their hand must be cut off. At one time, a Christian who wanted to be religious had to take a vow of poverty. Jains were not allowed to touch money — this was solved by having someone accompany them to carry their money for them. Jews could not work on the day of the Sabbath. For those who follow this rule today, it means they cannot turn on a light switch.

Fanaticism flourishes when religious concepts are put before human values. In returning to the values, we will see that much of the misery that has come into the world in the name of religion can be avoided. This identification of values does not require guilt and fear to be introduced. You will find guilt and fear used for control in the history of all the religious systems in the world, but such discipline is not needed today. At this time we need only to cultivate love and understanding. The timeless values are a deep caring for all life, a responsible attitude towards the planet, non-violence, compassion and love, friendliness and cooperation, generosity and sharing, integrity, honesty and sincerity, moderation in one's activity, service, commitment and responsibility, peace, contentment, enthusiasm. These values are the very foundation of social order, justice and progress. Human values are social and ethical norms common to all cultures and societies, as well as religions. They represent a melding of social progress and spiritual growth.

Within the religious fanaticism that has grown in the world, you will find a basic lack of understanding of other religions. A comprehensive study of various religions would support the broader view that one supreme and caring intelligence has expressed itself to different people at different times and in different ways. Fanaticism comes to people who feel insecure. This broader view gives a sense of belongingness while still allowing people to be well founded in their own tradition.

There are ten major religions in the world, six from the Far East and four from the Middle East. In the Far East, Hinduism is the oldest. Then came Buddhism, Jainism, Taoism, Shintoism and Sikhism. From the Middle East, Zoroastrianism is the oldest, and then came Judaism, Christianity and Islam. Three of the Middle Eastern religions are rooted in the Old Testament: Islam, Christianity and Judaism. In the Far East Shintoism and Taoism have completely separate sources. Buddhism, Jainism and Sikhism have roots in Hinduism.

Far Eastern religions with different backgrounds peacefully coexist; Middle Eastern religions with a common root have conflicts. The six religions of the Far East have peacefully coexisted and intermingled over the centuries. Buddhism and Taoism have so completely accepted each other that you can find statues of Buddha in Taoist temples. Hinduism accepts Jain and Buddhist thought. Contrarily, the religions of the Middle East with a common root have warred with each other. The brothers of the same house fight while friends live with each other in a coherent manner. When I was in Japan I met several Shinto priests and Buddhist monks. They told me a story of travelling with President Bush of America. He asked a Shinto priest what the population of Shintoists in Japan was. The priest said, "Eighty per cent." And he asked a Buddhist monk what the percentage of Buddhists was and the monk said, "Eighty per cent." President Bush said, "How could that be possible?" And they said, "It is possible! Buddhists go to Buddhist temples and Shinto temples and Shintoists also go to Buddhist temples and Shinto temples." In this story, we have a healthy model of cultures maintaining their identity and at the same time interacting with each other. We can find a similar model in India also. Within one family you will find Jains and Hindus and Sikhs. Individuals are free to choose whatever representation of Divinity they wish. They are not expected to adhere to the choice of the father or mother. This coexistence can happen when we put values first and symbols and practices second. Sometimes unexpected interconnections between religions are found.

If we look at the practices in Hinduism and Christianity, we see that Christianity is a bridge between Eastern Hinduism and Judaism. Many Roman Catholic practices found in the Hindu tradition are not found in Judaism, the root of Christianity. The use of beads is one example. Beads, called "*japamala*", are a part of Hinduism, Buddhism, Sikhism and Jainism. Catholics use rosary beads, but Judaism makes no use of beads. Another example is the use of incense, an ancient tradition found in the Hindu tradition and in Buddhism, Shintoism, Taoism as well as the Catholic church. There are other links: the use of bells, worship of the feminine representation of God, the presence of multiple altars and icons in both Hindu temples and Catholic cathedrals, food as a part of ritual, marking the forehead with ash, the keeping of holy water in churches and temples, and more.

Christianity is a bridge between Eastern and Western traditions. When we feel conflict between our own religion and others, it may be because we are holding on to the wrong thing. If I say, "Buddha is great" not simply because he is, but because I am a Buddhist, because I have a personal ego identification with the greatness of Buddha, then conflict arises. This ego identification with one's own tradition is a block to valuing other traditions. It leads to "My God is better than your God" way of thinking. Humans have a strong need for an identification — the need to be "someone" is part of our human nature. People will kill in order to preserve an identification they have made. We see this in the children in the United States who belong to gangs. They will kill to preserve the identity and the sense of belongingness that they gain from gang membership. We need to see that our highest identity is not that of denomination or nationality — or gender or culture or profession or group membership. First we are part of Divinity and secondly we are human beings and part of the human family. This identification can free future generations of religious fanaticism.

There are certain texts in the scriptures of every tradition that, when narrowly interpreted or misinterpreted, cause misunderstanding and problems. In the Christian gospel, Jesus says, "I am the only way. No one comes to the Father except through me." This statement is widely taken by Christians to mean that you cannot attain the Kingdom of Heaven unless you believe in Jesus. But Krishna and Buddha have also made such statements: "Come to me and me alone. I am the only way." How can we understand the seeming contradiction in the fact that the founders of three major traditions each have claimed that they are the only way? We need to step back and look at these statements from a different angle. There is one eternal and omnipotent God who is not limited in the way His truth has been expressed throughout the ages. The one Consciousness that created the world has enormous intelligence and caring for the world. It brings up whatever is needed at the time that it is needed. Can we think that God was not there for all people through all time? Can we limit the scope and mercy of God in this way? Another way to look at these "I am the only way statements" is that Jesus, Krishna and Buddha were saying the abstract cannot be approached directly, but only through the personal. The teacher, the enlightened one, comes to be a bridge for you so that you can move from that which you can see and know to that which is invisible and unknown, from that which is changing and impermanent to that which is imperishable.

There is one eternal and omnipotent God who is not limited in the way His truth has been expressed. Saying "I am the only way" is also a means of focusing attention. In every religion, there are words offered which bring this focus. Jesus said, "Those who have come before me are robbers and thieves." He meant, "You are thinking about the prophets who came before me and ignoring what is present." The prophets are stealing your minds and attention. I am here now. Come to me and me alone.

Don't look anywhere else. Krishna has spoken in this way also: "Look only here. I am the only one." And Buddha said, "I am the past, the present and the future. I come again and again in every age." The eternal Son of God has come more than once — He has manifested many times. In the guru's great generosity he returns again and again, bringing wisdom from age to age. We have many conflicting scriptural statements between religions and we also find contradictory scripture within each religion. As an example, Jesus is described as the only Son of God, but then instructs his followers to pray, "Our father in heaven." Is there one son or many sons? These things need to be looked into.

"I am the only way" means the teacher comes to be a bridge so that you can move from what is known to what is unknown. We hear that we need to be tolerant of other religions, but I say we shouldn't be tolerant. Tolerance means that you don't like something, but you will put up with it. Respect is a better word. Respectfulness is a quality of divine consciousness. When someone respects you, it is their generosity speaking, not your virtue. When you respect someone, it is a sign of your magnanimity. How much respect you give to people is a sign of your own value. When we find the commonality in all religions, then respect will come. Then we can peacefully coexist and build a harmonious environment. Every major tradition has made a contribution to wisdom. The message of love and service in Christianity is unparalleled. The message of meditation and the theory of mindfulness in Buddhism are unfathomable. The knowledge of universe and self and life in the Vedic tradition is unmatched. The theory of karma is without equal in the Jain tradition. It is not necessary to see one tradition as better than another. All the religions of the world belong to all the world's people. The Divine has brought forth knowledge in different parts of the world at different times. Each of us belongs to the Divine and can claim all that the Divine has given as our own.

Every major tradition has made a contribution to wisdom. Read the sacred scriptures of any tradition and see them from a new angle. They all lead you to the basic human values of love, compassion and joy. You will find no religion that does not advocate truth, peace, service, compassion and caring for life.

Q: What does it mean to be enlightened?

Sri Sri: Enlightenment is like a joke! It's like a fish searching for the ocean. Once upon a time, there was a congregation of fishes who got together to discuss who had seen the ocean. None of them could actually say they had seen the ocean. Then, one fish said, "I think my great-grandfather had seen the ocean!" A second fish said, "Yes, yes. I also heard about this." A third fish said, "Yes, certainly, his great-grandfather had seen the ocean." So they built a huge temple and made a statue of the great-grandfather of that particular fish. They said, "He had seen the ocean. He had been connected with the ocean."

Enlightenment is the very core of our being; going into the core of our self and living our life from there.

We all came into this world gifted with innocence, but gradually, as we became more intelligent, we lost our innocence. We were born with silence, and as we grew up, we lost the silence and were filled with words. We lived in our hearts, and as time passed, we moved into our heads. Now the reversal of this journey is enlightenment. It is the journey from head back to the heart, from words, back to silence; getting back to our innocence in spite of our intelligence. Although very simple, this is a great achievement. Knowledge should lead you to that beautiful point of "I don't know."

The completion of knowledge will lead you to amazement and wonder. It makes you aware of this existence. Mysteries are to be lived, not understood. One can live life so fully in its completeness, in its totality. Enlightenment is that state of being so mature and unshakable by any circumstance. Come what may, nothing can rob the smile from your heart. Not identifying with limited boundaries and feeling "all that exists in this universe belongs to me," this is enlightenment. Enlightenment is a state of being so mature and unshakable by any circumstance.

Un-enlightenment is easy to define. It is limiting yourself by saying, "I belong to this particular place," or "I am from that culture." It's like children saying, "My dad is better than your dad," or "My toy is better than your toy." I think most people around the world are stuck in that mental age group. Just the toys have changed. Adults say, "My country is better than your country." A

Christian will say, "The Bible is truth," and a Hindu will say, "The Vedas are truth. They are very ancient." Muslims will say, "The Koran is the last word on God." We attribute glory to something just because we are from that culture, not for what it is. If one could take credit for all that exists throughout the ages and feel as though "it belongs to me," then that is maturity. "This is my wealth because I belong to the Divine."

The Divine, according to time and space, gave different knowledge in different places. One becomes the knower of the whole universe and sees that, "all the beautiful flowers are all from my garden." The whole evolution of man is from being somebody to being nobody, and from being nobody to being everybody. Have you observed that young children have that sense of belonging, that oneness, that innocence? As we grow up we lose that innocence and become more cunning. The innocence of an ignorant man has no value, and the cunningness of an intelligent man also has no value. Enlightenment is a rare combination of innocence and intelligence, with words to express and, at the same time, being very silent. In that state, the mind is fully in the present moment. Whatever is necessary is revealed to you in such a natural and spontaneous way. You just sit and the song flows through you.

Q: Is enlightenment really possible for the average person?

The answer is "Yes, a big YES." Enlightenment is definitely possible for the ordinary individual. Actually, it is easier than for someone who thinks that they are special. You see, when someone thinks they are special, their ego becomes involved. "I am a great teacher or I am a great writer," that is only ego. The ego wants to be special and this may cause someone to get stuck for a long time. Whenever someone is ordinary, simple, innocent and natural, that is enlightenment. Enlightenment is your very nature. It is in you already, in a form of a seed. When you drop all the tensions and hang-ups and become natural, then it is right in your hand. We simply need to let go of the old patterns that are in the mind, just drop them. Then you see that something in you flowers and dawns. It is so beautiful. In my teachings there is a lot of focus on the breath because our breath plays a very important role. The breath is the connecting link between the inner world of the mind and the outer world of body and environment. You see, there are seven levels of existence: body, breath, mind, intellect, memory, ego and Being. Meditation works by bringing an effect from the level of Being to the mind. With the breath we bring this effect to the physical level as well.

You see, there is a rhythm in nature. Seasons come and go. Everything in life has a particular pattern and order. In your own body, there is a rhythm, too. You feel hungry at a certain time and sleepy at a certain time. The body has a particular rhythm. Life has a particular rhythm. Similarly, your breath also goes in a particular pattern. Your emotions move in a particular rhythm, as well as your thoughts. All these rhythms arise from your Being, which has its own rhythm.

In *Sudarshan Kriya*, we get into the rhythm of our Being and see how Being is permeating our emotions, our thoughts, our breath and our bodies. In a very short amount of time, every cell of the body becomes so alive and releases all the toxins and negative emotions it has stored from times past. Once again, we are able to smile from our hearts. It is very precious knowledge.

People who are trying to be what they are not become unnatural and create much more tension and stress. That is why one must go deep into the source of their nature, their Being, and come from there. You see, I don't say that you will never get upset again in life. If someone promises you that you will never get upset . . . it just is not true. You may still get upset, but the quality of your life will not be the same. You will not get so caught up in your emotions for long periods of time. People have found that after they do *Sudarshan Kriya*, that they are able to come back to themselves very quickly. Whatever mood comes up, they are able to let go and come back and enjoy much, much more.

CHAPTER THIRTEEN

THE
KNOWLEDGE SHEETS

Life energy, the consciousness has enormous potentialities, the power and the intelligence. It is this intelligence that knows, how tall each stem should be and where it shall be green or yellow, hard or soft. The seed has the whole structure of how the plant will develop.

GURU*JI* DOES NOT READ AT ALL. ONCE HE HIMSELF
had said that he could not read more than two pages of
any book as he either went into meditation or fell asleep!
On the other hand, he can, at the drop of a hat, give a
talk on any topic and come out with such profound gems
of wisdom framed in the most simple terms, that they
are accessible to anyone. Out of these impromptu talks
with disciples, were born a few years ago what is now
known as "knowledge sheets" which basically consists of
aphorisms, or condensed knowledge, on a particular topic.
I have always found it fascinating to watch Guru*ji*
formulating a knowledge sheet. It is usually a Wednesday
late afternoon or evening, where he sits with a group of
people and answers their queries on any one subject which
makes up the knowledge sheet. These knowledge sheets

are so unique that even though the subject is of a serious nature, the atmosphere is one of lightness and hilarity. In such simple words and with such eloquence, a short knowledge sheet is born, which is then faxed or e-mailed to more than four thousand *satsang* centres around the world where it is read. The demand for it has increased so much that they are now on the internet and some newspapers in India and Europe have also started publishing them regularly. I am including here some of the knowledge sheets which have been taken from the book, *An Intimate Note to the Sincere Seeker*, and *Celebrating Silence*.

Don't Label Yourself

Right away, stop judging yourself and labelling yourself and your expression of love.

You are clearly like a ripe fruit. We assume the Divine qualities and we do not analyse or cultivate them.

Love finds its expression spontaneously.

When the mango is ripe its colour changes and you can spot it out at a distance.

Being in Utter Love

Being in utter love inspires. It brings confidence in applying knowledge. The visible sign of utter love is an undying smile.

The Self knows neither sorrow nor death, yet in it flow all the relative events.

It is easy to be detached when you are not in love. Being in utter love, and yet undisturbed, caring yet not worried, persistent yet not perturbed, are all the obvious signs of the Self shining through.

Hide your dispassion and express your love.

By expressing your dispassion, you lose enthusiasm in life.

And by not expressing love you feel stifled.

Expressing dispassion may bring ego.

Hide dispassion in your heart like the roots of a tree.

A love that withstands rejection will be free from anger and ego.

A commitment that withstands humiliation will be one pointed and reach its goal.

Wisdom that withstands emotional turbulence will get integrated in life.

Faith that withstands a million chances of doubt will bring perfection.

Events that withstand Time become morals for millions.

What is the Purpose of Love?

Love in itself is the end not the means to something. A purpose is always related to something that has an end. The purpose of cooking is to eat. The purpose of comfort is to live. A tree blossoms, what is the purpose? Love itself is the end.

The purpose of everything is to be in love. The Guru is love. The Guru kindles such an unusual love, beyond fear, anxiety, hatred, greed, jealousy. Love that encompasses the whole universe.

What is the purpose of love?

The question itself is irrelevant.

Desire

All desires are for happiness. That is the goal of desire, isn't it? But how often does your desire lead you to the goal? Have you thought about the nature of desire ? It simply means joy tomorrow and not now.

Joy is never tomorrow. It is always now.

How can you really be joyful right now when you have desires?

Desire appears to lead you to happiness, but in fact it cannot. That is why desire is maya (illusion).

Ego

When is there ego?

1. When you don't get attention
2. When you seem to be losing attention
3. When you get attention

Ego causes heaviness, discomfort, fear, anxiety. Ego does not let love flow. Ego is separateness, non-belongingness, wanting to prove and possess. Ego can be transcended by knowing the Truth, by enquiring "Who am I?". Often, you feel contempt or jealousy towards someone who is egotistical. But rather you should have compassion or even pity.

There is also a positive aspect of ego. Ego drives you to do work. A person will do a job either out of compassion or out of ego. Most of the work in society is done out of ego. But in *satsang* work is done out of love. When you wake up and see that there is nothing to be proved and nothing to possess, ego dissolves.

Judgements and Good Company

Though you have heard "Don't judge", judgement comes unavoidably in day-to-day life. By the actions and behaviours of people you either approve or disapprove.

But always remember that everything is changing, and do not hold on to the judgement, otherwise it gets solidified like a rock. It brings misery for you and for others.

If judgements are lighter, like air, like a breeze, they bring in fragrance and then move away. Or they could bring a foul smell, then move away. But they should not stay forever.

Judgements are so subtle that you are not even aware of their existence. Judging or labelling someone as judgemental is also a judgement. Only in the state of Being, when you are full of love and compassion, can you ever be free from all judgements.

Yet the world cannot move without judgements. Until you judge something as good or bad you cannot do any action. If you see rotten apples in the market, you say, "no good". It is only the good ones that you will buy. If someone lies to you ten times, you think the next time he speaks it could also be a lie. A judgement happens automatically.

See the possibility that people and things can change at any time and don't hold on to judgement.

You need to judge your company. Your company can pull you up or pull you down. The company that drags you down towards doubt, dejection, blame, complaints, anger, delusion and desires is a bad company. The company that pulls you towards joy, enthusiasm, service, love, trust and knowledge is a good company.

When someone complains, first you listen, then you nod, then you sympathize, then *you* complain.

Dennis : I confess, you are absolutely right.

Robert : Join the party!

Sri Sri : Your company can create hell for you in heaven — or heaven for you in hell. Judge for yourself.........!

The Purpose of Life

Our first and foremost commitment in the world is to do *seva* or service.

If there is fear or confusion in your life it is because you lack commitment.

The very thought "I am here in this world to do *seva*," dissolves the "I" and when the "I" dissolves, worries dissolve. *Seva* is not something you do out of convenience or for pleasure. The ultimate purpose of life is to be of service.

An uncommitted mind is miserable. A committed mind may experience rough weather but will reap the fruits of its toil.

When you make service the sole purpose in life, it eliminates fear, brings focus in your mind and purposefulness, action and long-term joy...and maybe short-term problems!

Success

Q: How was yesterday's programme? Was it successful?

Sri Sri: There is no question of success if you have nothing to gain. There is nothing to gain if you have only come to give and serve. Success indicates non-supremacy. Success means what? It indicates that there are chances of failure. If something is supreme, there is nothing to lose. People running after success only exhibit their limitations.

Success means crossing a limit. To cross a limit you have to assume that you have a limit. Assuming a limit is underestimating yourself. If you have no boundaries, then where is your success? If you have limitless access, then there is no success. You don't say that you successfully drank a glass of water, because it is well within your capabilities. But when you do something that is beyond your perceived limits, you claim success.

When you realize your unboundedness, then no action is an achievement.

Anyone who claims to be successful only reveals his limitation. If you feel very successful, it means that you have underestimated yourself. All your gains can be smaller than you. Taking pride in any gains is belittling yourself.

Sheila: What if you feel that you are not serving successfully?

Sri Sri : When you serve others, you may feel that you have not done enough, but you will not feel that you have been unsuccessful. Real service is when you feel that you have not done enough.

Kai: You are not very successful! (laughter)

Sri Sri: I am just full!

Religion and Politcs

The role of religion is to make one righteous and loving, and politics means caring for people and their welfare. When religion and politics don't coexist, then you have corrupt politicians and pseudo-religious leaders.

A religious man who is righteous and loving will definitely care for the welfare of the whole population and hence become a true politician. And for a true politician to be righteous and loving he cannot but be religious. All the *avatars* and prophets have been caring for people and so were in politics. You can find many examples to this effect.

When religions restrict the freedom to worship and restrict modes of worship they become unsuitable for creating a harmonious society. When religion becomes all encompassing and gives full freedom to pray and worship in any manner — that religion will bring righteousness and peace in people and will be suitable for any society. People think politics and religion have to be kept separate because many religions did not give freedom to worship and did not care for all people equally. History has shown that religion has created conflict but irreligious societies (e.g., communism) have created chaos and corruption.

Today both religion and politics need reform. Religion has to become broader and more spiritual to allow freedom of worship and broader to encompass all the wisdom in the world. And politicians have to become more righteous and spiritual.

Karma

Some karma can be changed and some cannot.

When you prepare a dessert, if there is too little sugar or too little butter, too much or too little milk, it can all be adjusted, repaired. But once it is cooked, it cannot be reversed.

If buttermilk is sour, milk or salt can be added to make it drinkable but it can never be reversed back to milk.

Prarabdha karma cannot be changed. *Sanchita* karma can be changed by spiritual practices. *Satsang* burns the seed of all negative karma.

When you praise someone, you take on their good karma.

When you blame someone, you take on their bad karma.

Know this and surrender both good and bad karma to the Divine and be free.

Do it Until You Become It

Virtues have to be practised until they become your nature. Friendliness, compassion and meditation should continue as practices until you realize that they are your very nature.

The flaw in doing something as an act is that you look for a result. When it is done as your nature you are not attached to the result and you continue doing it.

An action that arises from your nature is neither tiring nor frustrating. For example, daily routines like brushing your teeth are not even considered actions because they are so integrated into your life. You do all this with doership. When *seva* is made part of your nature it happens without doership.

Q: When do you realize that compassion, seva and meditation are your nature?

Sri Sri: When you cannot be without them.

Wise men continue their practices just to set an example even though for them there is no need for any practices.

Faith is your Wealth

If you think your faith in God is doing a favour to God, then you are mistaken. Your faith in God or guru does nothing to god or Guru. Faith is your wealth.

Faith gives you strength instantly. Faith brings you stability, centredness, calmness and love. Faith is your blessing.

If you lack faith, you will have to pray for faith. But to pray, you need faith! This is a paradox.

People put their faith in the world, but the whole world is just a soap bubble. People have faith in themselves, but they don't know who they are. People think they have faith in God, but they really do not know who God is.

There are three types of faith:

(1) Faith in yourself: Without faith in yourself, you think, "I can't do this: this is not for me: I will never be liberated in this life."

(2) Faith in the world: You must have faith in the world or you can't move an inch. You deposit money in the bank with faith that it will be returned. If you doubt everything, nothing will happen for you.

(3) Faith in the Divine: Have faith in the Divine and you will evolve.

All these faiths are connected; you must have all three for each to be strong. If you start doubting in one, you will begin to doubt everything.

Bill: Atheists have faith in themselves and faith in the world, but not in God.

Sri Sri: Then they don t have complete faith in themselves — and their faith in the world cannot be constant because there

are always changes. Lack of faith in God, the world, or yourself
brings fear.

Faith makes you full — faithful!

Q: Was Buddha an atheist?

Sri Sri: A pure atheist is impossible to find. An atheist is one who does not believe in anything that is not concrete and tangible. Life is not all concrete and tangible. Nor is the universe. Whether it is business, science or art, they all involve a certain amount of guesswork, assumptions, imagination and intuition. All of them are ethereal in nature and are not tangible. The moment an atheist accepts, even remotely, a field that is unexplainable, he ceases to be an atheist. Any intelligent person cannot rule out the mystery in life and the universe and hence cannot honestly be an atheist! The so-called atheists are perhaps only denouncing certain concepts of God.

Q: Was Buddha an atheist?

Sri Sri: No in one sense because he professed emptiness which is very hard for an atheist to accept and yes in another sense because he did not profess concepts of God.

Jim: An atheist believes only what he can see but Buddha
said all that you see is not real.

Sri Sri: If only in present day atheists could be Buddhas...

CHAPTER FOURTEEN

A GLIMPSE INTO
ETERNITY

In the company of your friend, you lose your centredness. Your enemy puts you back in yourself. Your friend sympathizes with you and makes you believe in matter. Your enemy makes you feel helpless and take you to the spirit. So your enemy is your friend and your friend is your enemy. Krishna said to Arjuna, "One who is unfriendly every where — including to himself — his consciousness is stable and his awareness is established."

*I*T WAS WINTER AND THE GHATS WERE ALL DESERTED. There was no moonrise this time, only a tiny crescent on the horizon: Shiva's moon. Seven years later, on a cold misty December night, we were once again on the Ganges with Guru*ji*. In the distance, one could barely distinguish the outline of the ghats and the lights of Varanasi shivering in the dark, like little oil lamps. The atmosphere was magical as ever; again, someone started singing softly a *bhajan* and again Sri Sri closed his eyes, a mysterious smile on his face. Once more my soul soared high — but this time I knew where I was going: there, behind my heart, to a tiny point of warmth and light, of concentration and delight.

I looked back on the years that had elapsed since my first ride on the Ganges of Life with Guru*ji*. I had spent innumerable days with him, listened to him for hours, meditated with him, talked to him, travelled with him all over India. Teaching his Basic Course has been an enlightening experience, a boon and an honour. Time has flown, yet it has stood still; I have changed, but something in me, which is eternal, has remained the same: the same François, the same secret "I", unchanged at ten years of age, or fifty, or even eighty; the same "I" which passes from one life to another. A touch of Guru*ji* has put me in touch with my Self. After all these years, I have finally come to understand that we are all born with this innocence and love.

Yet the mystery — who is Sri Sri — has deepened over the years. Many people have strong certitudes: "He is Krishna", say some; "Shiva", think others; "an Avatar", I have heard others say. Yet for me, the nearest to truth would be to state that Sri Sri is an embodiment of Love. He is what we all really are, just more obvious. Coming near him is like being embraced in a cocoon of love, watching him always triggers love, being with him is being swept away by love, looking at him is feeling love for everyone. As he himself has said so many times, "Love is present in all creation. Everything is Love. But you have never related it in your life other than by name and form."

Suffice it to say that Sri Sri is a glimpse into eternity, a window to our inner Self; he is the smile that we all secretly carry in ourselves; he has come to take us from the religious to the spiritual, from fear to the innocence that has always been in us.

Come, sit in this boat and let it carry you to the other side. In joy and celebration.

Appendix 1

The Courses

As I grew in AOL, I quickly discovered that the Art of Living is a vast foundation which has centres in more than 140 countries and offers a variety of courses. Here is a sample of the infinite variety of courses which Sri Sri has devised.

Courses for Children

The world belongs to children; they are the ones who are going to shape the 21st century. Guru*ji* has bestowed utmost attention to the future generations and has the knack of teaching profound things in a playful manner.

Namrita remembers arriving at the *ashram* after a long and tiring bus journey from Pondicherry. She recounts, "it felt so good to be welcomed by all these smiling bright faces and after registering I was told to go for lunch. Walking towards the kitchen, I heard an ancient prayer being chanted by children in their young melodious voices and my feet hurried me towards this sound. I suddenly felt my tiredness fall away. Reaching there I grabbed hold of the first person I saw as I had to know who these children were and what they were doing! I was so drawn to these kids with their bubbling joy and tinkling laughter who looked so different from the children I was used to seeing in the cities ! I was told that all these kids were taking part in a camp called ART Excel. What was this camp was the next question that sprang up in my mind and lunch forgotten, I started talking to the teacher about what this programme was all about. Dinesh explained: This ART Excel programme (All Round Training in Excellence), is a course specifically designed for youngsters. Today we have seen how all over the world such a great percentage of teenagers are suffering from depression, drug addiction and violence. The ART Excel programme presents practical tools to alleviate tension, increase their focus and augment overall well-being . The eighteen-hour programme incorporates ancient Vedic knowledge within a practical framework that appeals to youth of all ethnic, racial and religious backgrounds. The programme helps teenagers drop their inhibitions, lethargy, shyness and unfriendliness. Teens develop a spirit of adventure which enables them to deal with the unexpected twists and turns, upsets and challenges life may bring. A typical weekend includes yoga postures, breathing techniques, meditation, and processes that reawaken the traditional value system of love, com-passion, peace, generosity, gratitude and grace. Another

ART Excel teacher, Sharmila, feels that 'hearts and minds are thus opened to the greater values of life. Teens leave happier, more self-aware, with an experience of mutual acceptance, sensitivity towards others and tools that they can use every day to deal with their emotions.'

"Translated into practical living this means that teens learn how to face their emotions and deal with them in positive and constructive ways, rather than blindly react to their environment. Techniques of profound relaxation enable teens to release stress caused by pressures at school and the demands of a tension-filled society. Once learned correctly, these techniques can be used in any place or situation to bring calmness, increase focus and augment mental clarity. Teens often comment that they use the knowledge of breathing taught on the course to decrease test anxiety and more easily recall their studies. Those who like to walk on the wilder side of life find an opportunity for self-reflection and moderation.

"I was very inspired and as time went on I became an ART Excel teacher and dicovered for my self the magic of this course and how a shy child like Archana blossomed during the camp. Activities throughout the course are designed to lead the participants into a closer understanding of themselves and others. Those with low self-esteem gain self-confidence in this safe, stimulating and nurturing setting. It is such a joy to watch them band together to help each other when someone is feeling depressed, angry or frustrated! Many a crisis has been averted just by having the loving support of peers."

Corporate Courses

Today, stress has become a way of life in the corporate world, because of increasing pressures to achieve and produce at a faster rate. These high levels of stress which are being experienced in the work place, regardless of earning capacity or status, create untold havoc on the functioning of the body and lead to blood pressure, heart problems and even cancer. Unless the quality of life is improved, not only will disappointment and frustration continue to interfere with creativity, productivity and harmonious interaction, affect both business and personal life, but the harm to the body will not be contained.

We met Ajit, an executive with an MNC, five years ago and our first impression was of a completely stressed-out person. He just could not relax and would fidget non-stop. Over the years, doing the different courses, beginning with the Corporate Course, there has been such a vast improvement in him that it is an inspiration in itself!

The Self Management Seminar is a proven method for improving the quality of life. It is a practical and effective training programme that can empower managers and employees to experience unshakable calmness and inner clarity in the midst of any challenge or crisis. Says Vinod Menon, one of the corporate AOL teachers: "The Self Management Seminar is based on innovative breathing techniques that permanently reduce stress and heighten one's mental clarity and awareness. These powerful techniques, which are easily learned and practised, improve concentration, enhance creativity and increase efficiency."

These techniques and processes taught during the seminar create fundamental changes in the lives of employees that are essential for transforming any work environment. The seminar also incorporates basic principles for effective living, emphasizing the essential human values that help individuals lead more fulfilling and productive lives. Ajit now teaches these courses that are customized to suit specific company needs and has seen people benefit in different ways, the most obvious being enhanced creativity and clarity of mind for executives and employees along with improved productivity and team efficiency. As stress reduces, he finds a greater commitment and job satisfaction in people who have done the seminar. Many participants felt that their health improved and there was a general feeling of well-being along with increased physical energy, heightened enthusiasm and improved self-esteem.

The Self Management Seminar is divided into four sessions and can be held over a weekend or during the week. Even the aeronautical world has benefited from the Corporate Courses, as William Hayden, Senior Systems Analyst, NASA tells us: "As an engineer I need to be both analytical and creative. Mental clarity and stamina are also essential. The Self Management Seminar has given me the tools to enhance these abilities. An additional plus is a better sense of health and well-being."

This Seminar offers specific breathing techniques that infuse the body with energy and harmonize the natural rhythms of the body, mind, and emotions. Due to the intensity and stress of the business environment, these natural rhythms get distorted. Experienced as burnout or ill health, this discord creates fatigue in the body and mind, creating mental and emotional imbalances, lowering one's productivity and efficiency.

The Art of Living Course for Depression

Depression is a disabling disease that takes the joy out of life for millions around the world — men, women, and children — regardless of race, income, or family background. Depression also contributes to the downward spiral of many diseases, from cancer and HIV to asthma and cardiovascular disease. Finding an effective treatment for depression is a global health concern. The Art of Living Course for Depression offers a variety of techniques that have been documented by independent medical studies to be effective in alleviating depression. These simple, yet powerful techniques have advantages over many other forms of treatment because they are free from negative side-effects, cut health care costs, and are easy to learn and practice in daily life.

Due to the often long-term and chronic nature of depression, Art of Living Courses for Depression usually run longer than regular Art of Living Course and are sometimes taught as in-residence programs.

The Art of Living Course for Conorary Heart Disease

It is common belief that stressful life events lead to the risk of Coronary Heart Disease (CHD). Anyone can develop CHD regardless of age, sex, race or ethnic backgrounds. Sometimes there may be no warning signs and symptoms and even if there are any, either they are not noticed or they are ignored. The history of CHD is higher in urban population than in rural population, which is a major cause for premature death.

When 3 risk factors like Hyper-Lipidemia (high fat & cholesterol content in blood), Hyper-tension and smoking are present in an individual the chances of heart attack is seven times higher whereas, when individually present the risk is two-fold. Whatever may be the risk factor, the basic pathology of CHD is deposition of LDL cholesterol (harmful cholesterol), fat and other substances on the walls of the coronary arteries. These deposits thicken the arterial walls and narrow the arteries, which will slow or block the flow of blood. Heart receives a constant supply of oxygen through blood any blockage of which may result in chest pain (Angina Pectoris) and Myocardial Infarction (heart attack) or even death. An individual can improve the quality of life by preventing the things harmful for health and by working on things that are good. Regular *Sudarshan Kriya* practice, *ujjai*, *pranayama*, and *bhastrika* can work wonders here.

Appendix 2

Medical References

1. *Stress-related Biochemical Effects of Sudarshan Kriya Yoga in Depressed Patients*, B N Gangadhar, N Janakiramaiah, B Sudarshan, K T Shety, National Institute of Mental Health and Neurosciences, 1999.

   Effects of Sudarshan Kriya Practice on Auditory Middle Latency Responses, B L Meti, NIMHANS Department of Neurophysiology, 1995.

   Sudarshan Kriya and Heart Rate Variability, N Janakaramaiah, NIMHANS Department of Psychiatry and Neurophysiology, 1996.

2. *Effects of Sudarshan Kriya in Dysthymic Disorders*, B L Meti, T R Raju, N Janakaramaiah, N Venkatesh, P J Murthy, B N Gangadhar, Departments of Neurophysiology and Psychiatry, NIMHANS 1996.

3. *Treatment Effects of Sleep Pattern Abnormalities in Melancholic Depression*, M G Harish, Unpublished dissertation submitted to National Board of Examinations (Psychiatry), New Delhi, 1997.

The Art of Living Course for the Patients with Multiple Sclerosis: *First Results*, D Kovacic, an unpublished report to the Institute for Rehabilitation of the Republic of Slovenia, 1999.

4. *Normalization of P300 Amplitude following Treatment in Dysthymia*, P J Naga Venkatesha Murthy, B N Gangadhar, N Janakiramaiah, and D K Subhakrishna. Biological Psychiatry, 1997: Vol. 42, pp. 740-743.

Therapeutic Efficacy of Sudarshan Kriya Yoga (SKY) in Dysthymic Disorderly, N Janakiramaiah, B N Gangadhar et al, NIMHANS Journal, January 1998, pp 21-28.

P300 Amplitude and Antidepressant Response to Sudarshan Kriya Yoga (SKY), P J Naga Venkatesha Murthy, N Janakiramaiah, et al, Journal of Affective Disorders, 1998, pp 45-48.

Effects of Sudarshan Kriya in Dysthymic Disorders, B L Meti, T R Raju, N Janakiramaiah, N Venkatesh, P J Murthy, B N Gangadhar. Departments of Neurophysiology and Psychiatry, NIMHANS. 1996.

Antidepressant Efficacy of Sudarshan Kriya Yoga (SKY) in Melancholia: A Randomized Comparison with ECT and Imipramine, N Janakiramaiah, B N Gangadhar, P J N Venkatesha Murthy, et al, Journal of Affective Disorders, 2000, Vol. 57, Issues 1-3, pp 255-259.

5. *Electrophysiological Evaluation of Sudarshan Kriya; An EEG, BAER, P-300 Study*, M Bhatia, A Kumar, N Bharadwaj, R M Pandey, V Kochupillai, All India Institute of Medical Sciences, New Delhi-29, India, 2001.

Appendix 3

Table 1
Effect of Sudarshan Kriya Practice on LIPID Profile & LIPID Peroxidation in Normal Individuals

Group (mg%)	Total Cholesterol Mean (SD)	TG (mg%) Mean (SD)	HDLc (mg%) Mean (SD)	LDLc (mg%) Mean (SD)	VLDL (mg%) Mean (SD)	MDA (nmole/ml) Mean (SD)	P Value
Before SKP	189.35 (37.89)	139.8 (73.78)	43.18 (7.16)	118.32 (37.92)	28 (14.81)	3.32 (1.27)	
7th Day SKP	168.62 (28.94)	160.22 (86.41)	46.56 (7.84)	91.76 (31.10)	31.98 (17.34)	2.0 (0.7)	

Table 2
Effect of Sudarshan Kriya Practice on LIPID Profile & LIPID Peroxidation in Normal Individuals

Group (mg%)	Total Cholesterol Mean (SD)	TG (mg%) Mean (SD)	HDLc (mg%) Mean (SD)	LDLc (mg%) Mean (SD)	VLDL (mg%) Mean (SD)	MDA (nmole/ml) Mean (SD)	P Value
Before SKP	189.35 (37.89)	139.8 (73.78)	43.18 (7.16)	118.32 (37.92)	28 (14.81)	3.32 (1.27)	
45th Day SKP	156.21 (26.33)	153.16 (73.71)	51.51 (7.73)	74.72 (26.52)	30.23 (14.78)	1.31 (0.38)	

Total number of subjects: 46

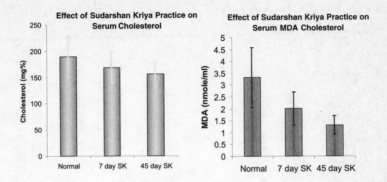

Effect of Sudarshan Kriya Practice on Serum Cholesterol

Effect of Sudarshan Kriya Practice on Serum MDA Cholesterol

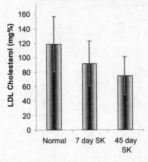

Effect of Sudarshan Kriya Practice on Serum LDL Cholesterol

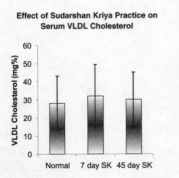

Effect of Sudarshan Kriya Practice on Serum VLDL Cholesterol

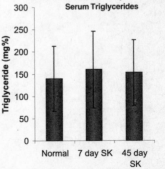

Effect of Sudarshan Kriya Practice on Serum Triglycerides